The Druid
Grove Handbook

A Guide to Ritual in the Ancient Order of Druids in America

Compiled and Edited
by John Michael Greer

The Druid Grove Handbook
A Guide to Ritual in the Ancient Order of Druids in America

Compiled and Edited by John Michael Greer

ISBN: 978-0-9791700-8-9

Greer, John Michael
The Druid Grove Handbook/John Michael Greer

First Edition: May 2011

Printed in the United States of America

9 8 7 6 5 4 3 2 1 0

Starseed Publications
2204 E Grand Ave.
Everett, WA 98201

Contents

Introduction

The Ancient Order of Druids in America (AODA) was founded in Boston, Massachusetts at the summer solstice of 1912 by Dr. James Manchester, an American Freemason, with a charter received from the Ancient Masonic Order of Druids (AMOD) in Britain. The order has been through plenty of ups and downs in the ninety-nine years since that time, and the rituals practiced by groves (chartered local groups) of AODA have been through many changes of their own over the same span.

Since ritual is an organic product of an order's history and experience, this is as inevitable as it is appropriate, and the rituals and information included here will one day be superseded in their turn. In the meantime, this book is meant to provide members of the order with a textbook for AODA ritual practice and grove organization, and I hope it will be useful to them as well as to others interested in the ritual work of a Druid order.

I owe hearty thanks to all those who helped make this book possible. First among those is Dr. John Gilbert, Archdruid Emeritus of AODA, who was instrumental in introducing me to the order and spent many hours with me reconstructing the old rituals and teachings in 2003 and 2004, when the two of us and a handful of others were struggling to bring the order back from the edge of extinction. Several individuals who contacted me at that time or later, and who expressed a wish to remain anonymous, provided me with collections of documents that filled in important gaps in the old rituals. Outside the AODA tradition, Philip Carr-Gomm, John Plummer, and Mark Stavish all gave me access to materials from older traditions of Druidry and esoteric spirituality that helped make sense of the often fragmentary AODA texts.

The members of AODA's Inner Grove working group patiently tested a number of draft rituals and gave me feedback on them, and useful feedback was also received from the members of AODA's Grizzly Peak, Oakstone, and Three Roads Groves. The other current Archdruids of AODA—Sara Greer, Gordon Cooper, and Siani Overstreet—have been consistently supportive in the process of revision that gave rise to this book, alongside their hard work on behalf of the order generally. My deepest thanks, however, must go to the members of AODA, who found its teachings and traditions relevant enough to their own lives to become part of its life and history. Without them, this book would be not only unwritten but useless.

/I\ John Michael Greer
Grand Archdruid, AODA
Spring Equinox 2011

Evolution of the AODA Grove Ritual

When the founders of the Druid Revival began to piece together their reimagination of Druidry in the early years of the eighteenth century, they had plenty of resources to hand. Their raw materials included Celtic lore, drawn predominantly from Welsh sources; classical Greek and Roman texts that mentioned the Druids, sometimes in passing, sometimes in detail; and a great deal of medieval and Renaissance mysticism that could be reworked to fit the needs of a Druidry in the dawn of the industrial era.

One thing they lacked almost completely, though, was information on the ways that the old Druids organized themselves. The classical writers mentioned here and there that Druids had some form of organization that crossed tribal boundaries: Caesar even mentioned an Archdruid whose authority extended in some sense over all of Gaul. Still, nothing was said about local or tribal Druid organization, how meetings were handled, how candidates for Druidic initiation were selected, or any of the other necessary details that an initiatory order needs to have in place in order to operate.

Fortunately, the founders of the Druid Revival had a resource to hand that was familiar to many of them, and could supply all of these things. Some scholars of their time even speculated that this source was actually descended from the ancient Druids. That source was Freemasonry.

1. The Masonic Foundations

The order of Free and Accepted Masons, to give it its proper title, emerged into the public eye in 1717, right around the time the Druid Revival was beginning to get under way. Though there are any number of exotic theories about the origins of Masonry, all the reliable evidence suggests that Masonry started out as exactly what it has always claimed to be, a medieval organization of master builders who absorbed a certain amount of mystical teachings from the sacred geometry and symbolism central to their work on the Gothic cathedrals.

3

Starting around 1600, masons' lodges in Scotland began to admit members who were not working stonemasons, but instead were local aristocrats interested in philosophy and esotericism. These "accepted Masons," as they were called, gradually became the majority in many lodges, and those lodges as gradually changed from craft guilds to social clubs with distinctive initiation rituals and symbolic teachings. By the beginning of the eighteenth century, lodges of Free and Accepted Masons had spread over much of Britain, and in 1717 four lodges meeting in London founded the first Grand Lodge of England.

One of the reasons why Freemasonry succeeded, where so many other societies of the same era failed, was a simple, flexible, and very efficient organizational form that the original Scottish stonemasons' lodges borrowed from the wider world of medieval guilds and religious confraternities. These lodges took their name from the temporary wooden buildings medieval stonemasons set up on building sites to provide a site for fine carving and tool storage. By 1717, though, a lodge had stopped being a building and become a group of Masons who met regularly, usually in a private room upstairs at a tavern.

The basic approach in place then is still practiced by Freemasons today. During the meeting, each officer has a specific place to sit: the Master, the head of the lodge, at one end of the room, symbolically in the East; the Senior Warden, second in command and responsible for discipline, on the opposite end, symbolically in the West; the Junior Warden, third in command and responsible for food and drink, at the middle of the wall to the Master's right, symbolically in the South. Each officer wears an emblem on a collar. Other members sit along the two side walls, with the space in the northeast traditionally set aside for newly entered apprentices.

Every meeting opens with an opening ceremony, and closes with a closing ceremony. In between, the members of the lodge attend to necessary business and confer the ceremonies of initiation that are most of a lodge's reason for existence. There are three such ceremonies in the oldest and most basic form of Freemasonry, the Craft or Blue Lodge: Entered Apprentice, Fellow Craft (sometimes called Companion), and Master Mason, the three degrees of the Craft, each with its distinctive symbolism. Once the old requirements of craft skill were set aside for accepted Masons, advancement from one degree to another came to be earned by memorizing a long catechism that recapped the events of the preceding initiation.

That was the basic organizational and ritual toolkit of Freemasonry. As it spread through British and, later, European and American society, it became the standard template for a vast number of organizations, some of them connected to Masonry in one way or another, others completely independent. Druid Revival groups were among those who borrowed Masonic methods for their own organizations and meetings. Just as the Masons turned the word "lodge" from a term for a building to a name for a local group, the Druids borrowed the term "grove" from accounts of the ancient Druids meeting in forest glades, and made it their standard term for a local Druid organization.

This sort of thing was standard practice in many lodges, clubs, and orders of the time. Still, there was a wild card in the relationship between Masonry and Druidry. A group of very popular and widely read writers at that time, some of them Masons and others not, insisted that the Freemasons were actually descended from the ancient Druids. All the available evidence today suggests that this notion is complete nonsense, but in the eighteenth and nineteenth centuries, a great many Masons and Druids believed it.

A complex history lies behind this notion. All through the eighteenth and nineteenth centuries, there was a booming market in romantic origin stories for Freemasonry. Most of the theories in circulation today—at least, most of the ones that don't have to do with extraterrestrial lizard people and similar products of twentieth century science fiction—come straight out of that age of doubtful scholarship and robust fantasy. Attempts to trace the origins of Masonry back to the Knights Templar, the Essenes, the ancient Egyptian priesthood, or the like were made popular by the intense class-consciousness of the time; it was simply too uncomfortable for upper-class Masons to admit that their cherished lodges traced their origins back to anything so grubby and working class as a bunch of medieval stonemasons.

The Druids were enlisted early and often in this quest for Masonic roots. The late eighteenth century was the heyday of Druid-Freemason speculations; authors of the time who produced books identifying Masonry with Druidry included such notables as American political pamphleteer Thomas Paine and John Cleland, better known as the author of the pornographic classic Fanny Hill. The equation was taken seriously enough that scholars know of at least two Masonic lodges at the end of the eighteenth century, one in Dublin and the other in upstate New York, that left Masonry altogether and redefined themselves as Druid organizations.

AODA also has its roots in this same tangle of Masonry and Druidry, but it emerged in a slightly more complicated way. According to Michel Raoult, whose 1984 book Les Druides: les Sociétés Initiatiques Celtiques Contemporaines (Monaco: Editions du Rocher, 1983) remains the only good history of the Druid Revival, the Ancient and Archaeological Order of Druids (AAOD) was originally founded in 1874 in London by Robert Wentworth Little. Little was an enthusiastic Freemason who served the United Grand Lodge of England as its secretary, and was also involved in a flurry of organizations, rites, and degrees on the fringes of Masonry. In 1866, for example, he was responsible for founding the Societas Rosicruciana in Anglia (Rosicrucian Society in England, SRIA), which went on to become the parent body of the famous Hermetic Order of the Golden Dawn.

According to Raoult, the AAOD existed for a while as an independent organization, admitting Masons and non-Masons alike. In 1886, after Little's death, it changed its name to the Ancient Masonic Order of Druids (AMOD), and expelled all its non-Masonic members, who at the time amounted to some two-thirds of the membership. The former members apparently tried to regroup under the old name, but their order seems to have gone out of existence somewhere around 1900; some later British Druids claimed a lineage from this group, but other than that it appears to have vanished without a trace.

The AMOD, however, proved to be a success, and in 1912 it chartered a daughter order in the United States, the Ancient Order of Masonic Druids in America (AOMDA). Like its parent body, the AOMDA was originally restricted in membership to Master Masons in good standing, and in its early days its groves met in Masonic lodge halls. Very little is known about its rituals or its activities, and indeed the AMOD and AOMDA have both left remarkably few traces. Both were small, to be sure, but there may be more to the matter than that.

In 2003, when I became Grand Archdruid of AODA, the handful of elderly members who were all that was left of the order had to think back to remember fragments of rituals which, at that time, had not been regularly performed for some years. One thing that became clear from their reminiscences is that the three degrees of the AODA as they recalled them had a great deal in common with Masonry. The names of the degrees were originally Apprentice Druid, Companion Druid, and Master Druid; the officers wore the emblems of the corresponding positions in a Masonic lodge, and numerous minor details of the AODA rituals were identical, or nearly so, to equivalent details in the corresponding Masonic rituals.

My speculation at this point—and it is only a speculation, though it explains all the available facts—is that the Masonic Druidry or Druid Masonry launched by Robert Wentworth Little was an attempt to recreate the "original Druid rituals" believed to have been the source of Freemasonry. Whatever the appropriateness of such borrowings in a British Masonic setting, the use of Masonic ritual forms outside Masonry was (and still is) strictly forbidden by American Masonic Grand Lodges, which struggled for most of a century and a half with copycat organizations and schismatic groups within Masonry.

If the Masons who founded the AOMDA worked a ritual that was based on Masonry, but that was not authorized by their Grand Lodges, they would have been thrown out of their Masonic lodges on their ears if they had been caught at it. This may account for the silence of the records, and the very faint traces left by the AOMDA in its earliest years.

2. The Gorsedd Inheritance

Freemasonry was not the only input to Little's original system, however. This became clear in a roundabout way in 2003, when I was being introduced to the AODA system.

In the course of conferring the AODA degrees on me, Archdruid John Gilbert communicated to me the Grand Druidic Word, which was then the password of the Third Degree (then called Master Druid) and was never to be spoken except in a grove open in that degree. The word he gave me was "Awen." Neither he nor any of the other surviving members of the order at that time knew what that word meant, and John was surprised to find that I not only knew the word but that it was used in public in most other Druid orders.

Behind that point of information lies a long history, beginning with one of the most influential figures in the Druid Revival. Edward Williams, better known by his Druid name Iolo Morganwg, conducted the first known public Druid ceremony in Britain since ancient times at Primrose Hill, London at the autumn equinox of 1798. A first-rate Welsh poet, the author of more than half the hymn lyrics in the present day Welsh Unitarian hymnal, and a devoted collector and more than occasional "improver" of Welsh folklore, Iolo set himself the task of reviving what was then the mostly moribund tradition of Welsh bardic poetry, complete with the guild structure and regular poetic competitions, or eisteddfodau, that formed the backbone of Welsh bardic culture in the Middle Ages.

In the process, he invented a set of rituals for gorseddau, or poetic assemblies, that he claimed were descended from the ceremonies of the ancient Druids. Those rituals have been published in their original form in J. William ab Ithel's The Barddas of Iolo Morganwg (York Beach, ME: Weiser Books, 2004). They include elements that have since become standard in nearly all Druid Revival orders, including the proclamation of peace at the beginning of the ceremony, the presentation of the sword, and the Universal Druid Prayer. All three of these features are found in current AODA ritual practice.

Another element of Iolo's system was a secret word concealed under the letters OIW, which was said to be the true name of God known only to the Bards of the island of Britain. According to material published online by Breton Druid circles, the actual word symbolized by OIW is in fact Awen, an archaic Welsh word meaning the spirit of inspiration. The truth of the matter will probably never be known outside of the Gorsedd Cymru and its daughter gorseddau in Brittany and Cornwall, but the word Awen has certainly been used as the OIW in a number of Druid Revival contexts, Welsh and otherwise, for at least a century. In the Order of Bards Ovates and Druids (OBOD), where I received my original Druid training, Awen is used as a chant in public as well as private ceremonies, and has an important role in the order's symbolism.

As far as anyone knows, Iolo intended his rituals and the teachings that went with them as nothing more radical than a context for Welsh poetic and cultural revival. Some of his students and followers, however, took things a good deal further. The gorsedd of Pontypridd, which was headed from the mid-nineteenth century straight through the 1930s by two colorful Welsh eccentrics, Evan Davies (druid name Myfyr Morganwg) and Owen Morgan (druid name Morien), became the center of a Druid religious movement that had followers in America as well as Wales, and attracted attention from the more esoteric end of the Masonic community; accounts of ceremonies at Pontypridd, for example, appear in early issues of the Proceedings of the Quatuour Coronati Lodge, the premier English journal of Masonic research. Exactly how the word Awen and other tidbits of Welsh Druid lore found their way into the AAOD, and from there into the AOMDA and AODA, is anyone's guess, but there were certainly channels available. It might have been something as simple as a Welsh Freemason who was a friend of Little's and an initiate of the Pontypridd gorsedd, and who passed on a few details to help Little build his Masonic Druid order.

3. Juliet Ashley's Revisions

After its founding, the AOMDA continued to operate in a very quiet way for several decades. The first major change occurred around

1944, when the order began to admit women as well as men; the rule that initiates had to be Master Masons was amended for this purpose to permit candidates to be recommended by a Master Mason if not one themselves. Sometime shortly after this change, Dr. Juliet Ashley was initiated into the order; she rose quickly through its rather sparse ranks and in 1952, after the death of Grand Archdruid Robert Hayes, was elected Grand Archdruid.

Ashley was an American occultist of what used to be the classic type. A student of Theosophy and the writings of quintessential American occultist Manly P. Hall, she made her living as a lay psychotherapist and hypnotist. She claimed to have studied with Carl Jung in Zurich before the Second World War, and to have received a charter for a branch of the Golden Dawn from Arthur Edward Waite while stopping in England on the way home in 1939. Whether or not these claims are correct is anyone's guess; it was common enough in the occult community of the time for the founder or head of an esoteric group to pad his or her resume with imaginary connections to famous figures, but ideas clearly inspired by Jung and the Golden Dawn do play a major role in all of the orders Ashley came to run, and notably the AODA.

One of the central principles of Jung's approach to symbols is the importance of fourfold patterns. Jung insisted that when a fourfold pattern showed up in the dreams of a patient under analysis, the pattern was a symbol of psychological wholeness, while a threefold symbol indicated that one of the four functions of the psyche was being repressed. It is probably not a coincidence that under Ashley's leadership, AODA shed the Masonic lodge arrangement with three principal officers (Master, Senior Warden, and Junior Warden), and took up a new arrangement with four principal officers, the four druids, in the four quarters of a circle.

It was at this time, similarly, that AOMDA groves began to place symbols of the four elements on the central altar, and to use them to purify the grove in the opening ceremony. This actually derives from a Golden Dawn custom. In the Neophyte Grade, the first level of Golden Dawn initiation, the lodge and then the candidate are purified with incense and water; that twofold purification was expanded, in the AOMDA and several other orders headed by Ashley around the same time, to a fourfold purification. Again, the similarity to Jung's ideas is unlikely to be coincidental.

Equally, the expansion of the AOMDA degree system from three initiations to four, with the addition of a Candidate grade prior to the first, Apprentice degree, seems to have been one of Ashley's innovations. That Candidate grade has no parallel in traditional Craft Freemasonry; the elegant ritual which was passed on to me, with its straightforward narrative and its links to what became the Sphere of Protection, was the ritual the elderly members of AODA remembered best in 2003, and it has needed the least reconstruction and emendation of any of the AODA ceremonies. If it was purely Ashley's work, as it seems to be, it will likely be one of her enduring contributions.

It is interesting to note that at least one of the changes Ashley brought to AODA was paralleled a little earlier, on the other side of the Atlantic, by Dion Fortune and her Fraternity of the Inner Light (FIL, now called the Society of the Inner Light). Fortune, like Ashley, was a lay psychologist, and her magical lodge system derived partly from Freemasonry—her teacher and initiator, Dr. Theodore Moriarty, was active in Co-Masonry, a schismatic branch of Masonry that admitted women as well as men—partly from Theosophy, and partly from the Hermetic Order of the Golden Dawn. In FIL lodges, however, the Masonic and Golden Dawn custom of having three principal officers was replaced by a structure with four principal officers, corresponding to the four quarters and the four elements.

One further ceremonial innovation seems to have come to the AOMDA rituals from Golden Dawn sources. In certain Golden Dawn ceremonies, a ritual called the Lesser Ritual of the Pentagram is used to banish unwanted influences from the lodge hall during the opening ceremony. This ritual involves among other things tracing pentagrams (five-pointed stars) in the four quarters of the space, while intoning divine names. In the Ashley-era AODA rituals as they were described to me, the symbols of the four elements—not pentagrams, but figures serving the same purpose—were traced in the four quarters of the grove during the opening ceremony. This was the seed from which eventually grew the Sphere of Protection ritual.

Alongside these ceremonial innovations came a great deal of new symbolic and instructional material drawn from the American occult scene of Ashley's time. I have not been able to find any record of what teachings the AOMDA may have had, if any, before her tenure as Grand Archdruid; there were unquestionably impressive Druid teachings in circulation in the American Druid scene, but many orders and degrees associated with Freemasonry then and now have nothing to offer but their traditional initiation ceremonies, and whatever instruction or insight the initiate can derive from those. AOMDA may have been doing something similar when Ashley joined it, though it was certainly not working along those lines by the time she finished with it.

Some of the material she brought into the order became woven into the lodge ritual and structure, and so is relevant here. Among the most important of these new elements were the Theosophical teachings concerning the Seven Rays. In Theosophy, these Rays are the basic creative energies of the cosmos, and a great deal of symbolism and teaching focuses on them and their application; Ernest Wood's useful book The Seven Rays (Wheaton, IL: Quest Books, 1979) is a good general guide to the Ray theory in that tradition.

The Seven Rays in Theosophy consist of a triad of primary principles—the red ray of power, the blue ray of love and wisdom, and the yellow ray of intellect; a central, equilibrating principle—the green ray of harmony—and a second triad of applied principles—the orange ray of science, the violet ray of religion, and the indigo ray of art, which is also the ray of magic. In the occultism of the mid-twentieth century, Ray theory had many applications and variations.

Another common and important bit of symbolism at the time, and for many centuries before, assigned the number four to the world of matter and the number three to the world of spirit. Just as there are four elements, four directions, four seasons, and so on in the material world, trinities, triads, and threefold patterns generally predominate—despite Jung's ideas—in many of the world's traditions of magic and mysticism. It seems to have been Ashley's insight that these two symbolic patterns could be related by way of the sevenfold pattern of the Rays, giving the system of directions, influences, and (in Theosophical terms) Rays found in AODA rituals today.

Essentially, the first four rays—the three primary rays and the central ray—were assigned to the four material elements: the ray of power to fire, the ray of wisdom and love to water, and the ray of intellect to air, while the central ray was assigned to earth. To the three applied rays were assigned three aspects of spirit—above, below, and within—which correspond also to the three currents of older Druid Revival energy work. These correspondences structure the AODA grove and many of its rituals, and are discussed in more detail later in this book.

Ashley's work was picked up and expanded by two later figures in the AODA. The first was Grand Archdruid Matthew Shaw, Ashley's successor in AODA's Northern Chair. Shaw, better known by his religious name Rhodonn Starrus (from Greek rhodon stauros, "Rose Cross"), was a minister in a small and schismatic offshoot of the Universalist Church that eventually became the Universal Gnostic Fellowship. He seems to have added little new material to the system assembled by Ashley, but systematized it and worked out at least some of the bugs in the very complex structure he inherited.

The second person to take up Ashley's work in a significant way is John Gilbert, who joined AODA in the 1950s and was a personal student of Ashley and Shaw. In the 1970s, as part of his Doctor of Divinity studies at Universal Seminary—a correspondence school founded by Shaw—Gilbert took the elemental banishings from the AODA grove opening ritual, combined it with other elements drawn from AODA and Golden Dawn sources, and created the Sphere of Protection ritual, now one of the basic building blocks of AODA ritualism and magical practice. While Gilbert never chose to advance to the position of Grand Archdruid, he had a major effect on the AODA tradition, not least because he was one of the few people who stayed with the order during and after the troubles in the 1990s that nearly put a period on the end of its history.

4. Recent Developments

When I was invited to join AODA in 2003, the order consisted of a small number of elderly members scattered around the United States. All of them had commitments to other esoteric orders, many of which seemed to have much better prospects for survival than an old-fashioned Druid Revival order that had torn itself to shreds in internal quarrels less than a decade before. Its records and archives had been destroyed by former Grand Archdruid Robert Johnson when he left the order in 1998, and most of what little paperwork had survived had gone into storage when his successor Betty Reeves went into a Colorado nursing home a few years later; despite repeated efforts following her death in 2008, the order has been unable to recover any of this material from her family.

That left the memories of a handful of members, notably Archdruid of the East John Gilbert, as the only remaining sources for the order's ritual. John and I worked together extensively in 2003 and 2004 to reconstruct the opening and closing rituals and the rituals of initiation. The main changes made at that time were, first, the removal of the last elements of specifically Masonic language and action from the rituals, and second, the revision of the passwords and symbols of the degrees. John Gilbert reconstructed the degree lectures from memory, and the new rituals were put into place in early 2004, as the order began to publicize itself and attract new members for the first time in many years.

As word got into circulation that AODA had a new Grand Archdruid, however, something unexpected happened. I was quietly contacted by nearly a dozen individuals in various corners of the country, not all of them present or former members of the order and most of them completely unknown to me. All of them said some variation on the words "Since you're the head of AODA now, you ought to have this." What "this" amounted to varied quite a bit from person to person, and much of it had no direct connection to AODA at all. Through this process I ended up in possession of quite a bit of material to which, to put things bluntly, I have no business having access; this included the complete initiation rituals and instructional

The Druid Grove Handbook

documents of a number of esoteric orders, not all of them defunct.

These papers joined two other collections of information relevant to Druidry that had been passed onto me on the condition that they remain private. The first was a collection of Druid material from the archives of the Order of Bards Ovates and Druids (OBOD), which was very generously given to me by OBOD's Chosen Chief Philip Carr-Gomm during a trip to Britain in 2003. The second was the rituals and instructional materials of the other esoteric orders that had been headed by Dr. Juliet Ashley and Rhodonn Starrus, which were communicated to me by John Gilbert in the course of my studies with him.

A great deal of this material was relevant to the AODA rituals in one way or another, but the sheer mass of it, and the disorganized state of much of it, made it almost impossible to sort out in a hurry. Much of my spare time between 2003 and 2010 accordingly went into studying the material I had been given, practicing the rituals and meditations that were part of various sections of it, and working up certain portions that were appropriate to publish into two books—The Druidry Handbook and The Druid Magic Handbook—and several other manuscripts and study courses that will be issued in various forms in the years to come. The decision to revise the AODA curriculum in 2010 made a new version of the rituals timely, and I have drawn extensively on the collections of material sent to me in preparing that new version, without using any material that belongs to existing orders—Druid or otherwise—or abusing the trust that was placed in me by those who passed on secret material.

Much of the resulting work is to be found primarily in the First, Second and Third Degree initiation rituals, which are not published in this book. Still, a few changes have been made to the opening and closing rituals, the Candidate initiation has been lightly revised, and I have also included here a set of rituals for the solstices and equinoxes—the four main festivals of the year in the original AODA system—which were present in embryo in the material I was given, and draw some of their symbolism from the rituals of the Hermetic Order of the Golden Dawn. In addition, a detailed discussion of the symbolism of the AODA grove and a few notes on training for grove officers have been added in the hope that they will be useful.

The Grove and its Symbolism

During AODA's heyday in the middle years of the twentieth century, its local groves and study groups established a regular pattern of meetings fairly similar to those of other esoteric lodges of the time. Regular meetings for all grove members were held four times a year, as close as possible to the solstices and equinoxes. These meetings were usually held in rented fraternal halls; each of them opened with the standard grove opening ceremony, took care of any necessary grove business, and performed a ritual celebrating the equinox or solstice then taking place.

It was common practice to proceed to an instructional lecture relevant to the work of the grove, followed by a poetry reading or musical performance suitable to the season; both these were kept to a reasonable length, so that the entire portion of the meeting between opening and closing was less than two hours. The meeting closed with the standard grove closing; afterwards a banquet was held either at the fraternal hall or a nearby restaurant, and there was plenty of time for members to talk to each other and the grove officers informally. These same activities, usually on a smaller scale, were also standard in AODA study groups, which differ from groves in that they are headed by a Second rather than a Third Degree initiate and can only confer the Candidate initiation.

These four quarterly meetings were thus the anchor points of each grove's and study group's work. Other meetings for all members could be held at any time, to welcome an official visitor from the Grand Grove, for example, or to host a workshop on some aspect of Druid practice. Aside from this, meetings were normally for initiation, and while these were open to all members of the appropriate degree, the only ones who usually attended were the grove officers performing the initiations, the candidates receiving them, and a few Second Degree members learning the initiation ceremonies. Many groves had a meeting scheduled once each month, right around the 21st, so that four meetings were assigned to the solstices and equinoxes and the other eight were for initiations or (if there were no candidates) practice for the lodge officers. Familiarity with the ritual work was understood to be essential for the effective performance of grove ceremonies.

At the core of all the ceremonial work of the grove or study group, however, was a set of interwoven symbolic patterns that also had to be studied carefully, and that helped to shape the consciousness of grove officers and members alike, providing meaning and context to the rituals. These patterns were woven into the teachings of the order, and used in solitary practice as well as grove work; understanding them is a necessary first step to working AODA ceremonial as it should be done.

1. The Circle and its Quarters

In its most basic geometry, a grove is a circle, with a center and four equally spaced points around the circumference specially marked out. All grove members thus sit in a circle, with the chairs of the officers at the four quarters. Symbolically, the grove is set in a natural clearing in the deep forest, surrounded by a circle of trees. It was in places like this, according to the classical authors, that the ancient Druids met to teach their students and celebrate their rituals. If the old AODA groves had owned their own meeting spaces — as far as I know, none ever did — mural paintings of forest scenes on the walls would likely have been used to help focus this imagery; many other orders did the like with the core imagery of their own systems.

The clearing in the forest is not the only symbolism defining the circle, however. At the same time, the circle of the Druid grove is also the circle of the heavens, traced out in space and time: in space, as the four directions; in time, as the four seasons of the year; by the combination of both with a traditional symbolism, as the circle of the four material elements. Onto this AODA's traditions map its more complex sevenfold elemental system. These details of symbolism are not trivia; they define and shape the experience of ritual work in a grove, and provide most of the mental imagery that is used in the grove to help energize that experience.

The center is the location of the altar. Traditionally, this was supposed to be made of a broad flat stone supported by two other stones set parallel to one another, the whole resembling one of the trilithons at Stonehenge; this was draped with a white cloth. Nowadays, for practical reasons, a small table or folding tray with a white altar cloth on it is usually used.

On the altar are six ceremonial objects: four cauldrons in the four quarters of the altar, a sickle, and a sprig of mistletoe or some other appropriate plant. The cauldrons contain emblems of the four elements: in the east, incense; in the south, a votive candle; in the west, water; in the north, salt. The cauldrons containing incense and the candle are typically half-filled with clean sand for the sake of heatproofing.

The sickle may have a gilt blade or one of plain steel; the handle should be of wood, bone, or some other natural material. It and the mistletoe are kept in the west, at the station of the Pendragon, before the grove is opened; they are placed on the altar during the opening ceremony, and removed during the closing ceremony. When on the altar, the concave side of the sickle faces one of the four directions, depending on the work to be done; the mistletoe lies across it, more or less at right angles.

The quarters are symbolically marked by four gateways, the Yellow Gate of the Rushing Winds in the east, the Red Gate of the Bright Flames in the south, the Blue Gate of the Mighty Waters in the west, and the Green Gate of the Tall Stones in the north. There are no physical gates at these locations, but gaps are left in the circle at east, south and west so that members of the Grove can enter and leave. The northern Gate has no gap.

Each Gate is assigned to certain members, who enter and leave through it. The Gate in the east is assigned to Candidates and guests; that in the south is assigned to Apprentices; that in the west is assigned to Companions and Adepts. The Gate in the north is not used by any incarnate person; through it pass the spiritual influences and entities that link the grove with the subtle powers of the Unseen that enliven and empower it.

There are seven chairs for the officers of the grove: one in the north, and two each, flanking the gateways, in the west, south, and east. As many other chairs as are needed for the members in attendance are placed between the gateways. Traditionally, Candidates and guests sit in the section of the circle between the northern and eastern gates; Apprentices sit in the section between the eastern and southern gates; Companions sit in the section between the southern and western gates, and Adepts sit between the western and northern gates.

2. The Officers

Each gate has a Druid as its guardian. In the north is the Chief Druid of the grove, who presides over the meetings and ceremonies of the grove. The north is the station of the element of Earth and the season of Winter; it represents the foundations, those things that endure, which it is the Chief Druid's work to preserve and uphold.

In the west is the Druid of Water, who is second in charge of the grove. The west is the station of the element of Water and the season of Autumn, the time of harvest; it represents the legacy of the year's labor. The Druid of Water therefore acts as the secretary of the grove, maintaining its records and correspondence with its members, other groves, and the Grand Grove.

In the south is the Druid of Fire, who is third in charge of the grove. The south is the station of the element of Fire and the season of Summer, the year's full abundance. The Druid of Fire therefore acts as the treasurer of the grove, safeguarding its funds and physical properties.

In the east is the Druid of Air, who is fourth in charge of the grove. The east is the station of the element of Air and the season of Spring, the time of beginnings and renewed light. The Druid of Air therefore acts as the instructor of the grove, communicating its teachings to new initiates and those working their way up through the sequence of degrees.

The Druids of Water, Fire and Air have assistants, the appointed officers of the grove. In the west with the Druid of Water is the Pendragon, who assists with the secretarial work. In the south with the Druid of Fire is the Almoner, who assists with the books and properties of the grove. In the east with the Druid of Air is the Herald,

The Druid Grove Handbook

who assists with the instructional program of the grove. All seven of the Grove officers also have specific roles in the opening, closing, seasonal, and initiation rituals.

The officers of a grove have specific garments and emblems that indicate their place and work in the grove:

The Chief Druid wears a green tabard over a white robe, and a white collar from which hangs the emblem of that office, an upright staff upon an equilateral triangle. He or she also carries a staff, which should be made of wood and may be carved or otherwise decorated as the Chief Druid and the Grove desire.

The Druid of Water wears a blue tabard over a white robe, and a white collar from which hangs the emblem of that office, a pair of quill pens crossed upon an equilateral triangle.

The Druid of Fire wears a red tabard over a white robe, and a white collar from which hangs the emblem of that office, a pair of keys crossed upon an equilateral triangle.

The Druid of Air wears a yellow tabard over a white robe, and a white collar from which hangs the emblem of that office, a pair of swords crossed upon an equilateral triangle. He or she also carries a sword, which should have a straight double-edged blade and a cross hilt; it represents Excalibur, the Sword of Arthur. It should have a sheath.

The Pendragon, Almoner and Herald wear tabards colored to match their respective directions, but do not wear collars. Each of them also carries a wooden staff topped with a sickle; the sickle may be gilded if possible, or alternatively made of brass. Stands to hold the staffs upright while the appointed officers sit are placed to the right of each appointed officer's chair.

It occasionally happens that a grove may need to open without the full complement of officers. This can be done, and in fact it is quite possible for a grove to be opened in full form by one person acting alone. If there is more than one person participating in the opening, the Chief Druid does the work assigned to that office and the remainder of the work is assigned as follows:

If there are two officers: One Assistant Druid sits in the south, and does the work of all officers other than the Chief.

If there are three officers: Druids of Air and Water in East and West; the Druid of Air does the work of that office and of the Herald and Almoner, the Druid of Water does the work of that office and of the Druid of Fire and the Pendragon.

If there are four to six officers: Druids of the four elements in their places; the Druids of Air, Fire, and Water each do the work of the appointed officer sitting in the same quarter, if the appointed officer is absent.

3. The Three Currents

Most of the world's spiritual traditions include the concept of a life force or subtle energy that is present in all things and gives them life and power. In the Welsh folk traditions from which the Druid Revival drew much of its lore, the term for this force is nwyfre (pronounced NOO-iv-ruh). While nwyfre is everywhere, it may be accessed most readily by way of certain currents or flows that are related to familiar natural phenomena. The two primary currents of nwyfre in AODA grove work, and in the AODA system generally, are the solar and telluric currents.

The solar current has its source in the sun and descends from above. It flows wherever light from the sky can reach, and even penetrates a short distance down into the soil. The other planets of the solar system reflect the solar current to earth just as they reflect the sun's light, and their cycles shape the flow of the solar current in ways that can be tracked by astrology and other magical traditions of time. The solar current's traditional symbols in myth and legend are birds such as the eagle, the hawk, and the heron. Magical writings sometimes call it aud or od, and in alchemy it is the Sun. Its primary symbol in Druid lore is the circle, representing the sun's orb, and it relates to the ray of Spirit Above. It is symbolically masculine, and its color is gold.

The telluric current takes its name from Tellus, an old name for the earth, and rises from below. It takes its form and character from the landscape the way the solar current takes its character from the turning planets; it is thus defined by space rather than time. The serpent and the dragon are the most common symbols of the telluric current in myth and legend. Its names in occult lore include the secret fire, the dragon current, and aub or ob, and in alchemy it is Mercury. Its primary symbol in Druid lore is the triangle, representing its fiery and transforming nature, and it relates to the ray of Spirit Below. It is symbolically feminine, and its color is green.

In the AODA grove, the solar and telluric currents are imaged respectively as descending from a point far above the altar and ascending from a point far below the altar. When they are brought into contact in the right way, they fuse and form a third current, which becomes the core energy of the grove ritual and the ceremonies of initiation.

This third current is called the lunar current. Unlike the solar and telluric currents, the lunar current does not exist naturally; it has to be made, out of the balanced fusion of the solar and telluric currents. The lunar current is called aur and or in occult writings. Its primary symbol in magical lore is the crescent moon, and its mythic symbols include the egg, the jewel, the sacred cup, and the child. It mediates between solar and telluric currents in the same way that the moon mediates between sun and earth. Its color is white.

With the formation of the lunar current at the center of the lodge, upon the top of the altar, the energies of the lodge take on their full sevenfold pattern: the four material elements at the four quarters, the solar and telluric currents above and below, and the lunar current at the center. This pattern is reinforced at the conclusion of the opening ceremony by the performance of the Sphere of Protection ritual by the Almoner. Regular individual practice of the Sphere of Protection assists the grove officers and members in helping to formulate these energies, and for this reason is a recommended practice for all grove members, and especially for the Chief Druid and the other officers.

The fusion of the solar and telluric currents that gives rise to the lunar current may only be performed in a place of balance. It is for this reason that the four elements and their powers are awakened first in the grove opening ceremony, and the three currents worked thereafter. This is also the reason why the grove closing ceremony includes a specific phase in which the powers of the elements are thanked and allowed to withdraw, but there is nothing equivalent for the three currents. The solar and telluric currents are always present, while the lunar current ceases to be present as soon as the stabilizing forces of the elements are withdrawn.

4. The Gates of the Year

The traditional AODA calendar, as already mentioned, had the solstices and equinoxes as its principal holy days. People who come to AODA nowadays out of the current Pagan scene tend to ask why the four "cross quarter" days—Imbolc, Beltane, Lammas, and Samhain—were not celebrated at that time to complete the eightfold year of modern Neopaganism. The answer is simply that the eightfold year did not exist before the early 1950s, when Ross Nichols of the Order of Bards Ovates and Druids and Gerald Gardner, the founder of modern Wicca, assembled it out of two earlier calendars.

Nobody anywhere in the world has been documented to have celebrated the eight festivals of the Neopagan year—all eight of them, that is, and only those eight—before that time. The Druid Revival from its start had focused its seasonal cycle on the solstices and equinoxes—the Alban Gates, as these were called, borrowing the term from the old Welsh names for these festivals. Gardner's Wicca (or as it was originally spelled, Wica) at first celebrated only the cross quarter days, which were referenced as a calendar cycle in a few old Irish sources.

The combination of the two cycles is elegant and entirely workable, and many modern Druid organizations have borrowed it; AODA groves at present are welcome to celebrate the cross quarter days if they wish to do so, and may celebrate any other days they wish on the same basis. The Alban Gates, however, must be celebrated by every AODA grove and study group to remain in good standing with the order.

At these times of the year, according to an archaic astrology still preserved in occult traditions, these are the gates through which celestial energies descend to Earth. Rituals performed at these times can draw on these currents of energy, and then radiate them outward into the human community and the world as a whole. The old belief that the fertility of fields and flocks depends on the proper performance of certain ceremonies at certain times of the year is considered to be a relic of this ancient tradition.

The solstices and equinoxes have their special role because they govern the relationship between Sun and Earth. At the equinoxes, the Sun is at the point in Earth's skies where the ecliptic—the apparent path of the Sun against the background of stars—crosses the celestial equator—the projection of Earth's equator into the heavens. This conjunction allows a direct flow of nwyfre to descend from Sun to Earth. The solstices, for their part, are the points at which the Sun's movement along the ecliptic takes it furthest from the celestial equator; it represents the peak of polarity between Sun and Earth; the point in time at which these two powers—and the solar and telluric currents that unfold from them—balance and complement each other most completely.

The four Alban Gates each correspond to one of the four Royal Stars of ancient astrology. The correspondence between gates and stars has changed with the precession of the equinoxes—the slow shift of the ecliptic relative to the celestial equator that takes their points of contact a degree back through the Zodiac every 72 years. The correspondences now used came into effect with the beginning of the Age of Aquarius in 1879, and will remain in effect for 4320 years, until the beginning of the Age of Sagittarius:

Alban Eiler (spring equinox)	Fomalhaut
Alban Heruin (summer solstice)	Aldebaran
Alben Elued (autumn equinox)	Regulus
Alban Arthuan (winter solstice)	Antares

The Royal Stars are conceptualized as watchers or guardians of the four gates of the year; in a terminology sometimes used in Druid writings, they are the four principal star logoi who establish the circle in which the Solar Logos and the Earth Spirit celebrate their marriage. They are visualized in this context in the solstice and equinox ceremonies.

5. Additional Symbolism

A range of additional symbolism from Celtic sources are woven into the grove rituals. The first of these is the Round Table itself. In an important sense, the grove is a Round Table; like the original, it has a circular form to point up the fact that all sit on the same level as equals. Starting from the grove as home and base, as Arthur's knights did from Camelot, members pursue their individual quests, returning to share fellowship and the knowledge gained on their journeys.

Another Arthurian symbol is Excalibur, the sword of King Arthur. This element entered Druid Revival ritual by way of Iolo Morganwg's bardic rituals and is common to most of the orders descended from the Revival. In AODA ritual, it appears in the opening, where its symbolic sheathing emphasizes the proclamation of peace to the four quarters, and in the closing, where the members pledge their service to the Earth.

Another symbol drawn from Iolo's work is that of the three rays of light, referred to in the opening ritual. These are the rays of knowledge, power, and peace, symbolically represented by the Druids of Air, Water and Fire respectively, and by green, blue, and white candles in the solstice and equinox ceremonies. They represent Awen, the creative presence of the divine.

Additionally, the Sphere of Protection with its sevenfold pattern of the elements plays a significant role in the opening ritual, and is alluded to in the closing. The Sphere invokes air in the east, fire in the south, water in the west, earth in the north, and calls on the power of these elements to invoke desired influences into the grove banish hostile influences away from it; it then invokes spirit in three modalities, arranged along the vertical axis of the grove—below (corresponding to the telluric current), above (corresponding to the solar current), and within (corresponding to the lunar current).

The Almoner is responsible for performing the Sphere of Protection ceremony in the opening, and retracing the banishing symbols in the four directions in the closing. Details of the Sphere

26

are included later in this book, on pages 65-71.

6. Grove Customs

In addition to the symbolism, a rich body of traditional lodge customs and practices shaped the way AODA groves functioned in the order's heyday. Most of this material came to AODA from its Masonic origins, but the same customs and practices can be found today in nearly all lodge organizations that have preserved any continuity with the past. Many of these traditions can seem very formal and arbitrary from today's perspectives. All of them, however, serve one or both of two purposes: they assist the magical work of the grove, and they also make the ordinary business of the grove go quickly and efficiently.

Central to grove work is the sense that the grove stands apart from the ordinary world. This is why each grove meeting is opened with a ritual in which the energies worked by the order are invoked, and closed with a ritual in which those same energies are released to their proper places. If at all possible, members should be in the lodge and in their seats by the time the grove opens. Once the opening ceremony begins, no one is admitted until it is finished.

When the grove is open, after the opening ceremony is concluded, anyone who wants to enter must give the password and sign of his or her degree to the appointed officer at the gate through which he or she enters, proceed to the south side of the altar, wait to be acknowledged by the Chief Druid, and then proceed to his or her seat. To leave the grove before the closing, a member repeats the process in reverse: he or she rises and goes to the altar, is acknowledged by the Chief Druid, goes to the gate assigned to his or her degree, and leaves.

While a grove is open, everyone present should be paying attention to what is being said and done. Speech and movement is kept to a minimum; normally only one person speaks or moves at a time, either as specified in the ritual or as directed by the Chief Druid. Cross-talk—that is, conversations between people in the grove, which are not part of grove business and are not shared with the rest of the grove—should be avoided, since it tends to distract both the people who engage in it and anyone else sitting nearby.

When a member wishes to speak in an open grove, he or she stands up, turns toward the Chief Druid, and waits to be recognzed. The Chief Druid responds by saying the member's name or (if an officer) title. The member bows slightly to the Chief Druid, speaks, and sits down when finished. No one but the Chief Druid is permitted to interrupt a member speaking in an open grove; the Chief Druid should use this right rarely, but should not hesitate to do so when a member is inappropriately monopolizing the floor or an argument is breaking out.

One rap with the Chief Druid's staff seats the members. Two raps instruct one officer, who is named immediately after the rap, to rise to his or her feet. Three raps instruct all present to rise. It was standard practice, whenever groves met in a place without wooden floors, to have a wooden board for the Chief Adept's staff to strike, so as to produce a clear audible rap.

The Druid Grove Handbook

Grove Opening Ceremony

(Before the grove is opened, all present dress in white robes and wear the colored cord belts of their degrees, and officers don their tabards and collars. The Chief Druid is seated in the north. Depending on the preferred practice of the grove, the other officers may also take their stations before the opening, or they may wait outside the grove and enter in procession. All members not holding office should be in place before the ritual begins.)

(The symbol * represents one rap with the staff.)

Chief Druid: (Rises from his/her chair) *** Druids, be attentive as I am about to open a grove of Druids in this place.

(If there is a procession, the officers enter in a line from the eastern gate in the following order: Herald, Druid of Air, Almoner, Druid of Fire, Pendragon, Druid of Water. The appointive officers carry their staffs upright before them, with the opening of the sickle facing ahead of them; Druid of Air carries the sword point upright in both hands in front of him/her. All officers circle around the grove once clockwise from east to east in the procession; Herald and Druid of Air leave the line at the east, Almoner and Druid of Fire at the south, and Pendragon and Druid of Water at the west. All officers stand in front of their chairs.)

Chief Druid: * (Chief Druid waits for all present to be seated, but remains standing.)

Chief Druid: ** Brother/Sister Druid of Air. (Druid of Air arises) What is the first duty of Druids assembled in the sacred grove?

Druid of Air: To proclaim peace to the four quarters of the world, for without peace our work cannot proceed.

Chief Druid: You will perform that duty.

(Druid of Air faces outward, to the east, and raises sword in scabbard horizontally, right hand on hilt, left on scabbard then draws the sword partway from the scabbard so that half the blade is visible.)

Druid of Air: Is there peace in the east?

All: There is peace.

(All concentrate on peace radiating out from the grove to bless

29

the land to the east. After a pause for this visualization, Druid of Air sheaths sword, lowers it, and proceeds to south, where the same process is repeated.)

Druid of Air: Is there peace in the south?

All: There is peace.

(The same visualization is performed. Druid of Air sheaths sword, lowers it, and proceeds to west, where the same process is repeated.)

Druid of Air: Is there peace in the west?

All: There is peace.

(The same visualization is performed. Druid of Air sheaths sword, lowers it, and proceeds to north, where the same process is repeated.)

Druid of Air: Is there peace in the north?

All: There is peace.

(The same visualization is performed. Druid of Air sheaths sword, lowers it, and proceeds to east, then turns to face the Chief Druid.)

Druid of Air: Chief Druid, the four quarters are at peace and our work may proceed. (Druid of Air sits.)

Chief Druid: ** Brother/Sister Herald. (Herald arises.) What is your place and your duty there?

Herald: My place in the grove is in the East Gate. My duty is to guard the Yellow Gate of Alban Eiler, the Gate of the Rushing Winds, to assist the Druid of Air, and to attend the work of the Grove.

Chief Druid: You will attend to that duty and guard the East Gate.(Herald sits.)

Chief Druid: ** Brother/Sister Almoner. (Almoner arises.) What is your place and your duty there?

Almoner: My place in the grove is in the South Gate. My duty is to guard the Red Gate of Alban Heruin, the Gate of the Bright Flames, to assist the Druid of Fire, and to attend the circle.

Chief Druid: You will attend to that duty and guard the South Gate. (Almoner sits).

Chief Druid: ** Brother/Sister Pendragon. (Pendragon arises.) What is your place and your duty there?

The Druid Grove Handbook

Pendragon: My place in the grove is in the West Gate. My duty is to guard the Blue Gate of Alban Elued, the Gate of the Mighty Waters, and to attend the altar.

Chief Druid: You will attend to that duty and guard the West Gate. (Pendragon sits.)

Chief Druid: ** Brother/Sister Druid of Air. (Druid of Air arises.) What is your station and your duty there?

Druid of Air: My station in the grove is in the east, where the Hawk of May hovers in the heights of morning and the Sun rises to illuminate the world. My duty is to invoke the Ray of Knowledge and purify the grove with air.

Chief Druid: You will attend to that duty and purify this grove and all within it with Air.

(Druid of Air goes to the altar, lights the incense, takes the cauldron to the East quarter and raises it high in both hands. All present visualize, as clearly as possible, the presence and nature of the element of Air in all its forms and manifestations. All imagine these flowing in from infinite distance from the East, into the cauldron of incense, forming a sphere of yellow light around it. From the yellow light emanates an intense feeling of lightness and freedom.

(The Druid of Air then travels once clockwise about the grove, symbolically purifying the Grove and its members with Air. As this is done, all present imagine the sphere of yellow light tracing and leaving a line of itself around the grove. The Druid of Air returns to the East, then takes the cauldron back to the altar, and returns to his/her station in the East. The cauldron on the altar is visualized by all to be still surrounded by its sphere of yellow light)

Chief Druid: ** Brother/Sister Druid of Fire. (Druid of Fire arises.) What is your station and your duty there?

Druid of Fire: My station in the grove is in the south, where the great Stag dwells in the summer greenwood and the Sun stands in the heights of heaven. My duty is to invoke the Ray of Power and purify the grove with fire.

Chief Druid: You will attend to that duty and purify this grove and all within it with fire.

(Druid of Fire goes to the altar, lights the lamp in the cauldron, takes the cauldron to the South quarter and raises it high in both hands. All present visualize, as clearly as possible, the presence and nature of the element of Fire in all its forms and manifestations. Imagine these flowing in from infinite distance from the South, into the cauldron of flames, forming a sphere of red light around it. From the red light emanates an intense feeling of power and clarity.

(The Druid of Fire then travels once clockwise about the grove, symbolically purifying the grove and its members with fire. As this is done, all imagine the sphere of red light tracing and leaving a line of itself around the grove. The Druid of Fire returns to the south, and then takes the cauldron back to the altar, and returns to his/her station in the South. The cauldron on the altar is visualized by all to be still surrounded with its sphere of red light.)

Chief Druid: ** Brother/Sister Druid of Water. (Druid of Water arises.) What is your station and your duty there?

Druid of Water: My station in the grove is in the west, where the Salmon of Wisdom dwells in the sacred pool and the Sun descends into the waters of autumn. My duty is to invoke the Ray of Peace and purify the grove with water.

Chief Druid: You will attend to that duty and purify this grove and all within it with water.

(Druid of Water goes to the altar, takes the cauldron to the West quarter and raises it high in both hands. All present visualize, as clearly as possible, the presence and nature of the element of Water in all its forms and manifestations. Imagine these flowing in from infinite distance from the West into the cauldron of water, forming a sphere of blue light around it. From the blue light emanates an intense feeling of receptivity and peace.

(The Druid of Water then travels once clockwise about the grove, symbolically purifying the grove and its members with water. As this is done, all imagine the sphere of blue light tracing and leaving a line of itself around the grove. The Druid of Fire returns to the south, and then takes the cauldron back to the altar, and returns to his/her station in the South. The cauldron on the altar is visualized by all to be still surrounded with its sphere of red light.)

Chief Druid: Brother/Sister Druid of Water, what is my station

32

and my duty?

Druid of Water: Your station is in the north, Chief Druid, where the great Bear guards the starry heavens and the Sun stands unseen at midnight. Your duty there is to govern this grove, holding the balance of the Three Rays, and to purify the grove with earth.

(The Chief Druid goes to the altar, picks up the cauldron of earth, takes it to the North quarter and raises it high in both hands. All visualize, as clearly as possible, the presence and nature of the element of Earth in all its forms and manifestations. Imagine these flowing in from infinite distance from the North, into the cauldron of earth, forming a sphere of green light around it. From the green light emanates an intense feeling of stability and fertility.

(The Chief Druid then travels once clockwise about the grove, symbolically purifying the grove and its members with earth. As this is done, all imagine the sphere of green light tracing and leaving a line of itself around the Grove. Chief Druid returns to the north and then takes the cauldron back to the altar, then returns to his/her station.

Chief Druid: *** It is my order that (Name) Grove of the Ancient Order of Druids in America be now open for the purpose of (purpose of meeting). Brother/Sister Druid of Air, you will invoke the blessing of the holy powers.

Druid of Air: Let us offer the words that have been the bond among all Druids:

(All join in repeating the words in boldface:)

Grant, O Holy Ones, thy protection

And in protection, **strength**

And in strength, **understanding**

And in understanding, **knowledge**

And in knowledge, **the knowledge of justice**

And in the knowledge of justice, **the love of it**

And in that love, **the love of all existences**

An in the love of all existences, **the love of earth our mother, and all goodness.**

Chief Druid: All please join me in repeating the sacred Word.

All: (chanting, with the syllables drawn out Ah-Oh-En:) AWEN,

AWEN, AWEN.

Chief Druid: * (All are seated.)

Chief Druid: ** Brother/Sister Pendragon, you will attend to the altar.

(Pendragon rises and takes sickle and mistletoe to altar, and arranges them at the center of the altar according to the work to be done:

• for a public ceremony or a Candidate initiation, the concave side of the sickle faces east;

• for an Apprentice initiation or any other ritual work done where nobody below the grade of Apprentice is present, it faces south;

• for a Companion initiation or any other ritual work done where nobody below the grade of Companion is present, it faces west;

• for an Adept initiation or any other ritual work done where nobody below the grade of Adept is present, it faces north.

(Once the sickle and mistletoe are arranged, Pendragon returns and is seated at the West Gate.)

Chief Druid: ** Brother/Sister Almoner, you will attend to the circle.

(Almoner rises and goes to the south of the altar, facing north, and begins the Sphere of Protection ritual with the Elemental Cross. He/she traces the symbols, invoking and banishing, in the four quarters, above and below, and finishes with the Circulation of Light. Almoner then returns to station and is seated at the South Gate.)

Chief Druid: ** Brother/Sister Herald. (Herald rises.) You will attend to the work of the Grove.

Herald: By direction of the Chief Druid, I proclaim this Grove open in due form for the purpose of (describes the work to be done at that meeting).

Grove Closing Ceremony

Chief Druid: *** Druids, be attentive as I am about to close a Grove of Druids in this place.

Chief Druid: * (Chief Druid waits for all present to be seated.)

Chief Druid: ** Brother/Sister Herald. (Herald rises.) Does any further work remain to us in the east?

Herald: (If there is no more business relating to the instructional program) Chief Druid, the work of the East is accomplished. (Herald sits.)

Chief Druid: ** Brother/Sister Almoner (Almoner rises.) Does any further work remain to us in the south?

Almoner: (If there is no more business relating to finances or grove properties) Chief Druid, the work of the South is accomplished. (Almoner sits.)

Chief Druid: ** Brother/Sister Pendragon. (Pendragon rises.) Does any further work remain to us in the west?

Pendragon: (If there is no more business relating to correspondence or records) Chief Druid, the work of the west is accomplished. (Pendragon sits.)

Chief Druid: ** Brother/Sister Druid of Air. (Druid of Air rises.) Our work being accomplished, the Sacred Grove is open to the east.

Druid of Air: (to Candidates and guests) Brother and sister Candidates and guests of the grove, if any of you has something to offer for the good of the grove, the order, or the Earth, the Sacred Grove is open to you.

(At this point, Candidates or guests who have anything to say rise, are recognized by the Chief Druid, speak and sit down.)

(When all who wish to speak have spoken, the Druid of Air rises, goes to the altar, takes up the cauldron of Air and carries it to the east. As s/he raises it, everyone visualizes healing and blessing energies streaming out from the cauldron, blessing every aspect of the element of Air.)

Druid of Air: With thanks I release the powers of Air to their rightful places. May peace prevail in the East.

(Druid of Air lowers the cauldron, takes it back to the altar, and returns to her station.)

Druid of Air: Chief Druid, peace prevails in my quarter. (Druid of Air sits.)

Chief Druid: ** Brother/Sister Druid of Fire. (Druid of Fire rises.) Our work being accomplished, the Sacred Grove is open to the South.

Druid of Fire: (to Apprentices) Brother and sister Apprentices, if any of you has something to offer for the good of the grove, the order, or the Earth, the Sacred Grove is open to you.

(At this point, Apprentices who have anything to say rise, are recognized by the Chief Druid, speak and sit down.)

(When all who wish to speak have spoken, the Druid of Fire rises, goes to the altar, takes up the cauldron of Fire and carries it to the south. As s/he raises it, everyone visualizes healing and blessing energies streaming out from the cauldron, blessing every aspect of the element of Fire.)

Druid of Fire: With thanks I release the powers of fire to their rightful places. May peace prevail in the south.

(Druid of Fire lowers the cauldron, takes it back to the altar, and returns to her station.)

Druid of Fire: Chief Druid, peace prevails in my quarter. (Druid of Fire sits.)

Chief Druid: ** Brother/Sister Druid of Water. (Druid of Water rises.) Our work being accomplished, the Sacred Grove is open to the west.

Druid of Water: (to Companions) Brother and sister Companions, if any of you has something to offer for the good of the grove, the order, or the Earth, the Sacred Grove is open to you.

(At this point, Companions who have anything to say rise, are recognized by the Chief Druid, speak and sit down.)

(When all who wish to speak have spoken, the Druid of Water rises, goes to the altar, takes up the cauldron of Water and carries it to the west. As he raises it, everyone visualizes healing and blessing energies streaming out from the cauldron, blessing every aspect of

The Druid Grove Handbook

the element of Water.)

Druid of Water: With thanks I release the powers of water to their rightful places. May peace prevail in the west.

(Druid of Water lowers the cauldron, takes it back to the altar, and returns to his station.)

Druid of Water: Chief Druid, peace prevails in my quarter.

Chief Druid: (rises and says to Adepts) Brother and sister Adepts, if any of you has something to offer for the good of the grove, the order, or the Earth, the Sacred Grove is open to you.

(At this point, Adepts who have anything to say rise, are recognized by the Chief Druid, speak and sit down.)

(When all who wish to speak have spoken, the Chief Druid rises, goes to the altar, takes up the cauldron of Earth and carries it to the north. As he raises it, everyone visualizes healing and blessing energies streaming out from the cauldron, blessing every aspect of the element of Earth.)

Chief Druid: With thanks I release the powers of earth to their rightful places. May peace prevail in the north.

(Chief Druid lowers the cauldron, takes it back to the altar, returns to his station.)

Chief Druid: Peace prevails in my quarter and throughout the Grove. Let any power remaining from our work be returned to the Earth for its blessing. (All present visualize the descent of excess energies through the center of the Grove to the center of the Earth.)

Chief Druid: *** It is my order that (Name) Grove of the Ancient Order of Druids in America be now closed until its next regular communication. Brother/Sister Druid of Air, you will invoke the Sword of Swords.

Druid of Air: (draws the sword and holds it high.) Behold this sword, the likeness of Excalibur, the Sword of Arthur, which rose from the waters and returned to them again. (Druid of Air advances to altar and lowers sword to extend horizontally a short distance above altar, with the blade held flat.)

Chief Druid: While this sword is unsheathed, as the kings of old pledged themselves to serve their land and people, will you swear with me your faithful service to the living Earth our home and mother?

(All present advance and place their right hands flat on the blade.)

All: We swear it! (All return to places.)

Chief Druid: Please join me in repeating the sacred Word.

All: (chanting, with the syllables drawn out Ah-Oh-En:) AWEN, AWEN, AWEN.

Chief Druid: Brother/Sister Pendragon, attend to the altar.

(Pendragon removes sickle and mistletoe from the altar and returns with them to the West Gate.)

Chief Druid: Brother/Sister Almoner, attend to the circle.

(Almoner goes to East and traces the banishing symbol of Air, then proceeds around the circle tracing banishing symbols of the elements in the quarters, then returns to the South Gate.)

Chief Druid: Brother/Sister Herald, you will proclaim this Grove closed.

Herald: By direction of the Chief Druid, I proclaim this Grove closed in due form.

Chief Druid: *

Initiation of a Candidate

(Before the Candidate's arrival, the anteroom is decorated with green boughs, if possible, to represent a clearing in the forest, and images of the Paths in the Forest are set up, if available. Cnce the Candidate arrives and is placed in the anteroom, the grove is opened in regular form, and all lights are turned down, with only the altar at the center of the grove illuminated. A yellow cord belt of appropriate length for the candidate is in readiness near the altar.)

(When all is ready, Herald proceeds to the anteroom to greet the Candidate.)

Herald: Be welcome in our Druid Grove. Come with me. I will be your Guide as you decide if you truly wish to become a Druid - or not.

(Herald takes Candidate by the left arm, leads Candidate into the Grove without giving signs or passwords, and proceeds to a position just South of the Altar, facing North.)

Herald: Please kneel at the altar, and call silently upon Deity, by whatever name or form you prefer, and ask for guidance as you decide whether to follow the Path of a Druid or not. When you are finished, please say aloud: "So mote it be," and await my return.

Candidate: (after praying) So mote it be.

(Herald comes to Candidate's side quickly, takes candidate by the left arm and helps her/him to arise.)

Herald: Come with me.

(Herald takes Candidate out through the eastern gate of the grove, and back to the anteroom.)

Herald: There are many paths in life. The path you have been following is that traveled by most people in this life. If you continue to follow it, you will work hard at honest work, raise a family if you will and Deity permits, and meet with your friends in the mead hall to tell tall tales and brag of worthless victories. Your life will be full of happiness and sadness, joy and peace, fear and anger, pain and suffering, love, apathy and hate. This is the Path of Ignorance and it leads you in a circle back to this Place of Decision time after time, life after life.

(Herald points to another path)

This is the well-worn path of successful people who as craftsmen and artisans earn their keep. They are more prosperous than ordinary working folk but they travel a rocky road of feast or famine. They enjoy happiness, peace, love and joy and they also suffer sadness, fear, anger, pain, hatred and apathy. Even though they are more prosperous than most, they also follow a Path of Ignorance.

(Herald points to another path)

This path covered with brambles and difficult to see is the Path of Leadership which few are willing to travel. It is a difficult path because leaders must clear the path so others may follow. This path leads to riches and privileges impossibleto imagine. Great leaders and various scoundrels follow this Path of Ignorance that also leads to sadness and happiness, anger and fear, pain and suffering, joy and peace, love, apathy and hatred.

(Herald points to several other paths)

These are all paths leading to success in this world and all of them are Paths of Ignorance. There is one more path before you. It is the Path of Knowledge. It is a difficult path, filled with hard work both within yourself and in this world you see before you. It is a path that tests your faith and determination constantly. It tests you in every relationship you enter and in every decision you make.

If you pass these tests, you will attain everything you can attain on any other path and you will attain knowledge. You will attain knowledge about the Sun and the Moon, the Earth and the sky, all the stars in the canopy of heaven and all the grains of sand on Mother Earth. You will attain knowledge of all the rocks, plants and animals. And you will attain the greatest knowledge of all, the knowledge of yourself.

If you fail these tests, you will return to this place, the Place of Decision so you may choose another path for your life. I will leave you here in this Place of Decision for you to decide which path you want to travel. Choose any path and I will still be your friend. But should you choose to discover the Path of Knowledge, return to the Grove and knock thrice upon the portal, and you will be admitted. I will await you until the Sun rises again in the East.

The Druid Grove Handbook

(Herald returns to grove, leaving candidate in anteroom. When Candidate knocks thrice on the portal of the grove, Herald goes to meet him/her.)

Herald: Be welcome once more in the Grove of the Druids. You have chosen to follow the Path of Knowledge for now. If that is your true intention, please kneel at the altar and once again ask for the guidance of Deity. When you have completed your silent prayer, signal as before by saying "So mote it be."

(Herald leads Candidate to altar, assists her/him to kneel, and then steps back a few paces.)

Candidate: So mote it be. (The Candidate remains kneeling.)

Chief Druid: (rises) As the Chief Druid of this Grove it falls to me to ask several questions concerning your intentions. Answer me truly. Is it your desire to follow the Path of Knowledge and learn the secrets of a Druid? If this is not your desire, say "No" and leave this Grove. The Herald will leave with you as a sign of our friendship. But if it is your desire, say "Yes" and we will continue.

(Candidate answers)

Chief Druid: The first steps of the Path of Knowledge will require you to learn from Earth and Sun and Moon for one year: to learn the ways of nature along the Earth Path, to celebrate the cycles of nature along the Sun Path, and to explore the mysteries of your own nature along the Moon Path. Are you willing to study these Paths for one year, to learn what they have to teach you? If you are not so willing, say "No" and leave this Grove. The Herald will leave with you as a sign of our friendship. But if you are so willing, say "Yes" and we will continue.

(Candidate answers.)

Chief Druid: The river that is Druidry has three great currents: the way of the Ovate, the student of nature; the way of the Bard, the student of the arts; and the way of the Druid, the student of the spirit. As part of your first steps along the Path of Knowledge, you will be required to choose one or more of these currents and undertake an exploration into their lore and wisdom. Are you willing to make such an exploration? If you are not so willing, say "No" and leave this Grove. The Herald will leave with you as a sign of our friendship.

But if you are so willing, say "Yes" and we will continue.

(Candidate answers)

Herald: You have answered "yes" to every question. If that is your intention you may proceed. If that is not your intention, you may not proceed and we will leave this sacred grove together as friends. Do you wish to proceed?

(Candidate answers. If all the answers have been affirmative, the ceremony proceeds.)

Chief Druid: Arise, Candidate (name).

(Herald assists in helping Candidate to his/her feet.)

Chief Druid: In the name and under the authority of the Grand Grove of the Ancient Order of Druids in America I proclaim you and welcome you as a Candidate of our Order. The Herald will assist you in donning your yellow cord belt.

(Herald helps Candidate put on cord belt.)

Now follow your guide through the realms of the elements, and listen carefully to the instruction you will receive.

(Herald takes Candidate by the left arm and proceeds to the Northeast part of the circle.)

Herald: Among Druids the place in which we meet is termed a grove. As a Candidate your place in this grove and every grove will be in the Northeast. Here you will be under the direction of the Druid of Air and close to the Eastern Gate through which you are to enter and leave the Grove. Only those of higher degrees may freely enter and leave by the other gates. As a Candidate your gate is always in the East.

(Herald and Candidate reach the East Gate.)

Herald: * (raps once with staff)

Druid of Air: Who comes here?

Herald: A duly initiated Candidate who seeks the mysteries of the Eastern Quarter.

Druid of Air: Be welcome, Candidate of our Order. This is the East Gate. It is the Yellow Gate of Alban Eiler, the Gate of the Rushing Winds, through which you may enter and leave this Grove as a Candidate. It is your privilege as a Candidate to pass through this Gate.

The Druid Grove Handbook

In our teachings, the mysteries of the elements are resumed in the Sphere of Protection, which is the first ritual you are instructed to learn and practice, and the key to most of the secrets of our Order. You will begin your instruction in that ritual here, in the east, by facing east. Trace a circle before you in the air clockwise, beginning thus at the uppermost point (does so), imagining it drawn in a line of yellow flame. Draw a line of yellow flame upwards from the uppermost point of the circle (does so) to complete the symbol of air. Imagine the circle filled with yellow flame and, pointing to the center, say, "I invoke the powers of air and ask for their blessing." Do this now.

(Candidate does so)

Druid of Air: Now trace the same symbol again, but draw the circle counterclockwise. Point to the center and say, "And with the help of the powers of air I banish all hostile influences from this place." Do this now.

(Candidate follows these instructions, prompted as necessary by Herald.)

Druid of Air: It is well. You may pass on to the quarter of fire.

(Herald and Candidate proceed to the South Gate.)

Herald: ** (raps twice with staff)

Druid of Fire: Who comes here?

Herald: A duly initiated Candidate who seeks the mysteries of the Southern Quarter.

Druid of Fire: Be welcome, Candidate of our Order. This is the South Gate. It is the Red Gate of Alban Heruin, the Gate of the Bright Flames, through which Druid Apprentices enter and leave this Grove. It is your aspiration as a Candidate to pass through this Gate.

You will continue your instruction in the Sphere of Protection here, in the south, by facing south. Trace a triangle point upwards before you in the air clockwise, beginning it thus from the uppermost point (does so), imagining it drawn in a line of red flame. Imagine the triangle filled with red flame and, pointing to the center, say, "I invoke the powers of fire and ask for their blessing." Do this now.

(Candidate does so)

Druid of Fire: Now trace the same symbol again, but draw the

43

triangle counterclockwise. Point to the center and say, "And with the help of the powers of fire I banish all hostile influences from this place." Do this now.

(Candidate follows these instructions, prompted as necessary by Herald.)

Druid of Fire: It is well. You may pass on to the quarter of water.

(Herald and Candidate proceed to the West Gate.)

Herald: *** (raps thrice with staff)

Druid of Water: Who comes here?

Herald: A duly initiated Candidate who seeks the mysteries of the Western Quarter.

Druid of Water: Be welcome, Candidate of our Order. This is the Blue Gate of Alban Elued, the Gate of the Mighty Waters, through which the Druid Companions and Druid Adepts enter and leave this Grove. It is your task as a Candidate to learn from those who pass through this gate.

You will continue your instruction in the Sphere of Protection here, in the west, by facing west. Trace a triangle point downwards before you in the air clockwise, beginning it thus from the lowermost point (does so), imagining it drawn in a line of blue flame. Imagine the triangle filled with blue flame and, pointing to the center, say, "I invoke the powers of water and ask for their blessing." Do this now.

(Candidate does so)

Druid of Water: Now trace the same symbol again, but draw the triangle counterclockwise. Point to the center and say, "And with the help of the powers of water I banish all hostile influences from this place." Do this now.

(Candidate follows these instructions, prompted as necessary by Herald.)

Druid of Water: It is well. You may pass on to the quarter of Earth.

(Herald and Candidate proceed to the North Gate.)

Herald: **** (raps four times with staff)

Chief Druid: Who comes here?

The Druid Grove Handbook

Herald: A duly initiated Candidate who seeks the mysteries of the Northern Quarter.

Chief Druid: Be welcome, Candidate of our Order. This is the North Gate. It is the Green Gate of Alban Arthuan, the Gate of the Tall Stones, through which only the Ever-Living Ones, our guardian spirits and the messengers of Deity, may enter and leave this grove. It is your duty as a Candidate to offer due reverence to those who pass through this gate.

You will continue your instruction in the Sphere of Protection here, in the north, by facing north. Trace a circle before you in the air clockwise, beginning it thus at the lowermost point (does so), imagining it drawn in a line of green flame. Draw a line of green flame downwards from the lowermost point of the circle (does so) to complete the symbol of earth. Imagine the circle filled with green flame and, pointing to the center, say, "I invoke the powers of earth and ask for their blessing." Do this now.

(Candidate does so)

Chief Druid: Now trace the same symbol again, but draw the circle counterclockwise. Point to the center and say, "And with the help of the powers of earth I banish all hostile influences from this place." Do this now.

(Candidate follows these instructions, prompted as necessary by Herald.)

Chief Druid: It is well. You may pass on to the altar, the heart of the grove, to learn the mysteries of Spirit.

(Herald and Candidate proceed back to the East Gate, then to the altar.)

Herald: We return to the place of beginnings, and then to the center of this grove. This is the place of the Orange, Violet, and White Gates of the Spirit. In the depth of the Earth stands the Gate Below and the Ray of Power. In the heights of heaven stands the Gate Above and the Ray of Knowledge. In the center of all stands the Gate Within and the Ray of Peace. These three rays of light are always present in the grove, and in any other place where you may be, for by them all things came into being.

You will complete your instruction in the Sphere of Protection here, at the center. In any grove in which you do not preside, you will approach the altar always from the south. Trace a circle in the air over the altar top before you, imagining it drawn in orange flame, and say: "I invoke the powers of Spirit Below and ask for their blessing." Do this now.

(Candidate does so.)

Now trace a circle in the air above you, imagining it drawn in violet flame, and say: "I invoke the powers of Spirit Above and ask for their blessing." Do this now.

(Candidate does so.)

Now touch your heart, imagining white radiance shining out in all directions, and say, "I invoke the powers of Spirit Within. May a Sphere of Protection be established about me now and always." Do this now.

(Candidate does so. Herald and Candidate then proceed to the northeast quarter of the grove.)

Herald: This Sphere of Protection will protect you from harm and deception this day. You will be given written instructions on how to perform this ritual daily to protect yourself and any place you may be. It will keep you safe while you study the things you have promised to study and learn. Our blessings go with you on your journey, and the help of those who pass through all four gates of the Grove will be available to you should you need it. Study and learn no matter what may befall you. Take your place in the Northeast among your brother and sister Druids.

(Candidate is seated in the Northeast. Any remaining work is done, and then the grove is closed in the usual form.)

The Druid Grove Handbook

Spring Equinox Ceremony

(The grove is opened in the usual way; the altar and grove may be decorated with spring flowers or other decorations appropriate to the season. After the opening, the Almoner places three tall unlit candles on the altar: a green candle in the east, a white candle in the south, and a blue candle in the west. These represent the Three Rays of Light. Almoner then returns to place. Each of the appointive officers has a small taper or long match that can be used to convey fire from the lamp at the south of the altar to one of the candles.

Chief Druid: * The Spring Equinox has arrived, and the Sun and Earth renew the bonds that unite them. In this time of balanced powers, let us invoke the blessings of all the holy ones upon the grove, the order and the Earth.

Druid of Water: In the world of nature the winter has ended and the Sun has completed half his long journey toward the north. The streams are full of water from the melting snow and the spring rains; sap rises in the trees and flowers begin to bloom. Birds return from their winter dwellings far to the south as life wakes from its time of sleep.

Druid of Fire: The ancients knew this season as the seedtime of the year, not only for the husbandman and the herdsman but also for those who stand at the gates between the Seen and the Unseen. They recognized at this time the power of the thought held in the mind's clarity and the word spoken upon the wind's breath; they called down wisdom from the Sun and called up power from the Earth to illuminate their minds.

Druid of Air: Therefore our work begins from the quarter of Air.

Chief Druid: **

(Herald rises and, during the following words, advances to the altar.)

Druid of Air: East;
Druid of Water: West.
Druid of Air: Air;
Druid of Water: Water.

47

Druid of Air: The realm of the Mind;

Druid of Water: The realm of the Heart:

Herald: May they enter into the great harmony.

(Herald lights the green candle on the altar, then returns to place and sits down.)

Chief Druid: **

(Almoner rises and, during the following words, advances to the altar.)

Druid of Fire: South;

Chief Druid: North.

Druid of Fire: Fire;

Chief Druid: Earth.

Druid of Fire: The realm of the Spirit;

Chief Druid: The realm of the Body.

Almoner: May they enter into the great harmony.

(Almoner lights the white candle on the altar, then returns to place and sits down.)

Chief Druid: **

(Pendragon rises and, during the following words, advances to the altar.)

Druid of Air: The realm of the Winds;

Druid of Fire: The realm of the Flames

Druid of Water: The realm of the Waves

Chief Druid: The realm of the Stones:

Pendragon: May they enter into the great harmony.

(Pendragon lights blue candle on altar, returns to place and sits down.)

(Druid of Air rises and advances to the altar, takes the cauldron of incense, and returns to the east, then faces eastwards, and holds up the cauldron, as though in offering.)

Druid of Air: By the hawk of May in the heights of morning, I invoke the air and the spirits of the air! May their blessings be with the grove, the order and the Earth during the season to come.

(All imagine a blazing star at the zenith, almost infinitely far above the grove; this is Fomalhaut, the Royal Star governing the ceremony. When this image is well established, Druid of Air takes

48

the incense cauldron back to the altar, replaces it, and returns to station.

(Druid of Fire then rises and advances to the altar, takes the cauldron of fire, and returns to the south, then faces southwards and holds up the cauldron, as though in offering.)

Druid of Fire: By the white stag of the summer greenwood, I invoke the fire and the spirits of the fire! May their blessings be with the grove, the order and the Earth during the season to come.

(All imagine a ray of light descending from the star at infinite height to the golden sphere of the Sun, blazing at zenith above the grove, high above but much closer than the star. When this image is well established, Druid of Fire takes the cauldron of fire back to the altar, replaces it, and returns to station.)

(Druid of Water then rises and advances to the altar, takes the cauldron of water, and returns to the west, then faces westwards and holds up the cauldron, as though in offering.)

Druid of Water: By the salmon of wisdom who dwells in the sacred pool, I invoke the water and the spirits of the water! May their blessings be with the grove, the order and the Earth during the season to come.

(All imagine the ray of light descending further from the blazing Sun to the sphere of the full Moon standing at zenith above the grove, high above but much closer than the Sun. When this image is well established, Druid of Water takes the cauldron of water back to the altar, replaces it, and returns to station.)

(Chief Druid then rises and advances to the altar, takes the cauldron of earth, and returns to the north, then faces northwards and hold up the cauldron, as though in offering.)

Chief Druid: By the great bear who guards the starry heavens, I invoke the earth and the spirits of the earth! May their blessings be with us and with all the world during the season to come.

(All imagine the ray of light descending from the shining Moon all the way to the Sphere of Protection you established around the temple. The entire Sphere is seen to be filled with rainbow-colored light, which radiates outward in all directions. When this image is well established, Chief Druid takes the cauldron of earth back to the altar, replaces it, and then returns to station.)

Chief Druid: Please join me in repeating the sacred Word.

All: (chanting, with the syllables drawn out Ah-Oh-En:) AWEN, AWEN, AWEN.

Chief Druid: In this season of spring may the Sun send forth his rays of blessing; may the Earth receive that blessing and bring forth her abundance. In this sacred time of balanced powers, in this sacred space in the midst of the elements, we invoke the union of Sun and Earth, that the land may be made fruitful and that all who desire the light shall find it. Let us meditate on the turning of the year and the gifts the coming season brings to all.

(A brief period of meditation follows. Chief Druid then raps once, and instructs the Herald to announce the lecture, if one is to be given, and the poetry reading or musical performance, if one is scheduled. Thereafter, the grove is closed in the usual way.)

The Druid Grove Handbook

Summer Solstice Ceremony

(The grove is opened in the usual way; the altar and grove may be decorated with summer greenery or other decorations appropriate to the season. After the opening, the Almoner places three tall unlit candles on the altar: a green candle in the east, a white candle in the south, and a blue candle in the west. These represent the Three Rays of Light. Almoner then returns to place. Each of the appointive officers has a small taper or long match that can be used to convey fire from the lamp at the south of the altar to one of the candles.

Chief Druid: * The Summer Solstice has arrived, and the Sun and Earth manifest the polarities of being. In this time of balanced powers, let us invoke the blessings of all the holy ones upon the grove, the order and the Earth.

Druid of Water: In the world of nature spring's promise has given way to summer's fulfillment and the Sun now stands at his highest point in the sky, preparing for his long journey into darkness. The land is mantled in green as every growing thing bends its strength toward the harvest. Life rejoices in the golden afternoon of the year even as it makes its preparations for the cold months to come.

Druid of Fire: The ancients knew this season as the year's bright summit, and waited in their stone circles for the fiery sign of midsummer sunrise, the seal of harmony that unites the turning worlds. They recognized at this time the power of destiny born from the innermost self and the kindling flame of the awakening spirit; they turned their faces to the Sun and set their feet upon the Earth to accomplish the work of their wills.

Druid of Air: Therefore our work begins from the quarter of fire.

Chief Druid: **

(Herald rises and, during the following words, advances to the altar.)

Druid of Fire: South;
Chief Druid: North.
Druid of Fire: Fire;
Chief Druid: Earth.

Druid of Fire: The realm of the Spirit;

Chief Druid: The realm of the Body.

Herald: May they enter into the great harmony.

(Herald lights the green candle on the altar, then returns to place and sits down.)

Chief Druid: **

(Almoner rises and, during the following words, advances to the altar.)

Druid of Air: East;

Druid of Water: West.

Druid of Air: Air;

Druid of Water: Water.

Druid of Air: The realm of the Mind;

Druid of Water: The realm of the Heart:

Almoner: May they enter into the great harmony.

(Almoner lights the white candle on the altar, then returns to place and sits down.)

Chief Druid: **

(Pendragon rises and, during the following words, advances to the altar.)

Druid of Fire: The realm of the Flames;

Druid of Water: The realm of the Waves;

Chief Druid: The realm of the Stones;

Druid of Air: The realm of the Winds:

Pendragon: May they enter into the great harmony.

(Pendragon lights blue candle on altar, returns to place and sits down.)

(Druid of Air rises and advances to the altar, takes the cauldron of incense, and returns to the east, then faces eastwards, and holds up the cauldron, as though in offering.)

Druid of Air: By the hawk of May in the heights of morning, I invoke the air and the spirits of the air! May their blessings be with the grove, the order and the Earth during the season to come.

(All imagine a blazing star at the zenith, almost infinitely far above the grove; this is Aldebaran, the Royal Star governing the ceremony. When this image is well established, Druid of Air takes the incense cauldron back to the altar, replaces it, and returns to station.

(Druid of Fire then rises and advances to the altar, takes the cauldron of fire, and returns to the south, then faces southwards and holds up the cauldron, as though in offering.)

Druid of Fire: By the white stag of the summer greenwood, I invoke the fire and the spirits of the fire! May their blessings be with the grove, the order and the Earth during the season to come.

(All imagine a ray of light descending from the star at infinite height to the golden sphere of the Sun, blazing at zenith above the grove, high above but much closer than the star. When this image is well established, Druid of Fire takes the cauldron of fire back to the altar, replaces it, and returns to station.)

(Druid of Water then rises and advances to the altar, takes the cauldron of water, and returns to the west, then faces westwards and holds up the cauldron, as though in offering.)

Druid of Water: By the salmon of wisdom who dwells in the sacred pool, I invoke the water and the spirits of the water! May their blessings be with the grove, the order and the Earth during the season to come.

(All imagine the ray of light descending further from the blazing Sun to the sphere of the full Moon standing at zenith above the grove, high above but much closer than the Sun. When this image is well established, Druid of Water takes the cauldron of water back to the altar, replaces it, and returns to station.)

(Chief Druid then rises and advances to the altar, takes the cauldron of earth, and returns to the north, then faces northwards and hold up the cauldron, as though in offering.)

Chief Druid: By the great bear who guards the starry heavens, I invoke the earth and the spirits of the earth! May their blessings be with us and with all the world during the season to come.

(All imagine the ray of light descending from the shining Moon all the way to the Sphere of Protection you established around the temple. The entire Sphere is seen to be filled with rainbow-colored light, which radiates outward in all directions. When this image is well established, Chief Druid takes the cauldron of earth back to the altar, replaces it, and then returns to station.)

Chief Druid: Please join me in repeating the sacred Word.

All: (chanting, with the syllables drawn out Ah-Oh-En:) AWEN, AWEN, AWEN.

Chief Druid: In this season of summer may the Sun make manifest the mystery of Light. May the Earth reflect that manifestation in the mystery of Life. In this sacred time of balanced powers, in this sacred space in the midst of the elements, we invoke the Sun in his glory, the Earth in her richness, and the harmony that unites them, that the unity of all being may be made manifest. Let us meditate on the turning of the year and the gifts the coming season brings to all.

(A brief period of meditation follows. Chief Druid then raps once, and instructs the Herald to announce the lecture, if one is to be given, and the poetry reading or musical performance, if one is scheduled. Thereafter, the grove is closed in the usual way.)

Autumn Equinox Ritual

(The grove is opened in the usual way; the altar and grove may be decorated with autumn leaves and fruit, or other decorations appropriate to the season. After the opening, the Almoner places three tall unlit candles on the altar: a green candle in the east, a white candle in the south, and a blue candle in the west. These represent the Three Rays of Light. Almoner then returns to place. Each of the appointive officers has a small taper or long match that can be used to convey fire from the lamp at the south of the altar to one of the candles.

Chief Druid: * The Autumn Equinox has arrived, and the Sun and Earth renew the bonds that unite them. In this time of balanced powers, let us invoke the blessings of all the holy ones upon the grove, the order and the Earth.

Druid of Water: In the world of nature summer has given way and the Sun has descended from the heights of heaven into the south. The leaves of the trees blaze with orange and red as the fields turn harvest gold. The cries of the geese sound overhead as they begin their long journey toward their winter homes. Squirrels leap from branch to branch as they prepare for the long cold months to come; the sound of clashing antlers rings through the woods as stags test their strength before the watchful eyes of does.

Druid of Fire: The ancients knew this season as the harvest time of the year, not only for those who gathered in the sheaves and led the cattle down from summer pastures but also for the wise whose harvest is the lore of past ages and the whispers of the Unseen. They recognized at this time the power of the desire cherished in the heart's silence and the bonds that reach from person to person like the sea uniting shore with shore; they called down power from the Sun and called up wisdom from the Earth to illuminate their hearts.

Druid of Air: Therefore our work begins from the quarter of Water.

Chief Druid: **

(Herald rises and, during the following words, advances to the altar.)

Druid of Water: West;

Druid of Air: East.

Druid of Water: Water;

Druid of Air: Air.

Druid of Water: The realm of the Heart;

Druid of Air: The realm of the Mind:

Herald: May they enter into the great harmony.

(Herald lights the green candle on the altar, then returns to place and sits down.)

Chief Druid: **

(Almoner rises and, during the following words, advances to the altar.)

Chief Druid: North;

Druid of Fire: South.

Chief Druid: Earth;

Druid of Fire: Fire.

Chief Druid: The realm of the Body;

Druid of Fire: The realm of the Spirit:

Almoner: May they enter into the great harmony.

(Almoner lights the white candle on the altar, then returns to place and sits down.)

Chief Druid: **

(Pendragon rises and, during the following words, advances to the altar.)

Druid of Water: The realm of the Waves;

Chief Druid: The realm of the Stones;

Druid of Air: The realm of the Winds;

Druid of Fire: The realm of the Flames:

Pendragon: May they enter into the great harmony.

(Pendragon lights blue candle on altar, returns to place and sits down.)

(Druid of Air rises and advances to the altar, takes the cauldron of incense, and returns to the east, then faces eastwards, and holds up the cauldron, as though in offering.)

Druid of Air: By the hawk of May in the heights of morning, I invoke the air and the spirits of the air! May their blessings be with the grove, the order and the Earth during the season to come.

(All imagine a blazing star at the zenith, almost infinitely far above the grove; this is Regulus, the Royal Star governing the ceremony. When this image is well established, Druid of Air takes the incense cauldron back to the altar, replaces it, and returns to station.

(Druid of Fire then rises and advances to the altar, takes the cauldron of fire, and returns to the south, then faces southwards and holds up the cauldron, as though in offering.)

Druid of Fire: By the white stag of the summer greenwood, I invoke the fire and the spirits of the fire! May their blessings be with the grove, the order and the Earth during the season to come.

(All imagine a ray of light descending from the star at infinite height to the golden sphere of the Sun, blazing at zenith above the grove, high above but much closer than the star. When this image is well established, Druid of Fire takes the cauldron of fire back to the altar, replaces it, and returns to station.)

(Druid of Water then rises and advances to the altar, takes the cauldron of water, and returns to the west, then faces westwards and holds up the cauldron, as though in offering.)

Druid of Water: By the salmon of wisdom who dwells in the sacred pool, I invoke the water and the spirits of the water! May their blessings be with the grove, the order and the Earth during the season to come.

(All imagine the ray of light descending further from the blazing Sun to the sphere of the full Moon standing at zenith above the grove, high above but much closer than the Sun. When this image is well established, Druid of Water takes the cauldron of water back to the altar, replaces it, and returns to station.)

(Chief Druid then rises and advances to the altar, takes the cauldron of earth, and returns to the north, then faces northwards and hold up the cauldron, as though in offering.)

Chief Druid: By the great bear who guards the starry heavens, I invoke the earth and the spirits of the earth! May their blessings be with us and with all the world during the season to come.

(All imagine the ray of light descending from the shining Moon all the way to the Sphere of Protection you established around the temple. The entire Sphere is seen to be filled with rainbow-colored light, which radiates outward in all directions. When this image is well established, Chief Druid takes the cauldron of earth back to the altar, replaces it, and then returns to station.)

Chief Druid: Please join me in repeating the sacred Word.

All: (chanting, with the syllables drawn out Ah-Oh-En:) AWEN, AWEN, AWEN.

Chief Druid: In this season of autumn may the Sun send forth his rays of blessing; may the Earth receive that blessing and bring forth her abundance. In this sacred time of balanced powers, in this sacred space in the midst of the elements, we invoke the union of Sun and Earth, that the land may be made fruitful and that all who desire the light shall find it. Let us meditate on the turning of the year and the gifts the coming season brings to all.

(A brief period of meditation follows. Chief Druid then raps once, and instructs the Herald to announce the lecture, if one is to be given, and the poetry reading or musical performance, if one is scheduled. Thereafter, the grove is closed in the usual way.)

The Druid Grove Handbook

Winter Solstice Ceremony

(The grove is opened in the usual way; the altar and grove may be decorated with winter greenery or other decorations appropriate to the season. After the opening, the Almoner places three tall unlit candles on the altar: a green candle in the east, a white cand_e in the south, and a blue candle in the west. These represent the Three Rays of Light. Almoner then returns to place. Each of the appointive officers has a small taper or long match that can be used to convey f_re from the lamp at the south of the altar to one of the candles.

Chief Druid: * The Winter Solstice has arrived, and the Sun and Earth manifest the polarities of being. In this time of balanced powers, let us invoke the blessings of all the holy ones upon the grove, the order and the Earth.

Druid of Water: In the world of nature the harvest is cver and the Sun has descended to the place of his death and rebirth. Cold blows the wind, and colder still lie the snow and the bare earth and the bare black branches of the trees beneath the bright stars; ice rimes the edges of the streams and breath bursts white from the lips. Only those creatures that cannot sleep the winter away pace through the silence of the winter days and wait for the coming of spring.

Druid of Fire: The ancients knew this season as the end and beginning of the year, and waited in their stone circles for the first light of the newborn sun, the promise of the new year yet to come. They recognized at this time the power of patience and the wisdom of the world beneath the turning stars, the lessons woven by countless seasons into bone and sinew and sense; they gazed with renewed wonder on the pale Sun and the cold Earth as they awaited the common destiny of all material things

Druid of Air: Therefore our work begins from the quarter of Earth.

Chief Druid: **

(Herald rises and, during the following words, advances to the altar.)

Chief Druid: North;
Druid of Fire: South.

Chief Druid: Earth;

Druid of Fire: Fire.

Chief Druid: The realm of the Body;

Druid of Fire: The realm of the Spirit:

Herald: May they enter into the great harmony.

(Herald lights the green candle on the altar, then returns to place and sits down.)

Chief Druid: **

(Almoner rises and, during the following words, advances to the altar.)

Druid of Water: West;

Druid of Air: East.

Druid of Water: Water;

Druid of Air: Air.

Druid of Water: The realm of the Heart;

Druid of Air: The realm of the Mind:

Almoner: May they enter into the great harmony.

(Almoner lights the white candle on the altar, then returns to place and sits down.)

Chief Druid: **

(Pendragon rises and, during the following words, advances to the altar.)

Chief Druid: The realm of the Stones;

Druid of Air: The realm of the Winds;

Druid of Fire: The realm of the Flames;

Druid of Water: The realm of the Waves:

Pendragon: May they enter into the great harmony.

(Pendragon lights blue candle on altar, returns to place and sits down.)

(Druid of Air rises and advances to the altar, takes the cauldron of incense, and returns to the east, then faces eastwards, and holds up the cauldron, as though in offering.)

Druid of Air: By the hawk of May in the heights of morning, I invoke the air and the spirits of the air! May their blessings be with the grove, the order and the Earth during the season to come.

(All imagine a blazing star at the zenith, almost infinitely

The Druid Grove Handbook

far above the grove; this is Antares, the Royal Star governing the ceremony. When this image is well established, Druid of Air takes the incense cauldron back to the altar, replaces it, and returns to station.

(Druid of Fire then rises and advances to the altar, takes the cauldron of fire, and returns to the south, then faces southwards and holds up the cauldron, as though in offering.)

Druid of Fire: By the white stag of the summer greenwood, I invoke the fire and the spirits of the fire! May their blessings be with the grove, the order and the Earth during the season to come.

(All imagine a ray of light descending from the star at infinite height to the golden sphere of the Sun, blazing at zenith above the grove, high above but much closer than the star. When this image is well established, Druid of Fire takes the cauldron of fire back to the altar, replaces it, and returns to station.)

(Druid of Water then rises and advances to the altar, takes the cauldron of water, and returns to the west, then faces westwards and holds up the cauldron, as though in offering.)

Druid of Water: By the salmon of wisdom who dwells in the sacred pool, I invoke the water and the spirits of the water! May their blessings be with the grove, the order and the Earth during the season to come.

(All imagine the ray of light descending further from the blazing Sun to the sphere of the full Moon standing at zenith above the grove, high above but much closer than the Sun. When this image is well established, Druid of Water takes the cauldron of water back to the altar, replaces it, and returns to station.)

(Chief Druid then rises and advances to the altar, takes the cauldron of earth, and returns to the north, then faces northwards and hold up the cauldron, as though in offering.)

Chief Druid: By the great bear who guards the starry heavens, I invoke the earth and the spirits of the earth! May their blessings be with us and with all the world during the season to come.

(All imagine the ray of light descending from the shining Moon all the way to the Sphere of Protection you established around the temple. The entire Sphere is seen to be filled with rainbow-colored

61

light, which radiates outward in all directions. When this image is well established, Chief Druid takes the cauldron of earth back to the altar, replaces it, and then returns to station.)

Chief Druid: Please join me in repeating the sacred Word.

All: (chanting, with the syllables drawn out Ah-Oh-En:) AWEN, AWEN, AWEN.

Chief Druid: In this season of winter may the Sun make manifest the mystery of Light. May the Earth reflect that manifestation in the mystery of Life. In this sacred time of balanced powers, in this sacred space in the midst of the elements, we invoke the Sun in his glory, the Earth in her richness, and the harmony that unites them, that the unity of all being may be made manifest. Let us meditate on the turning of the year and the gifts the coming season brings to all.

(A brief period of meditation follows. Chief Druid then raps once, and instructs the Herald to announce the lecture, if one is to be given, and the poetry reading or musical performance, if one is scheduled. Thereafter, the grove is closed in the usual way.)

Training for Grove Ritual

Grove ritual is, among other things, a performing art, and like any other performing art it requires a certain amount of training and practice if it is to be performed in a way that will have the intended effects on those present. The ceremonies already presented in this book thus need to be treated by the Chief Druid and officers of a grove in much the same way that musicians treat a piece of music. This parallel may be taken very far; just as musicians must first learn how to play their instruments, and then focus on the details of how to play any particular piece of music, participants in Druid ritual must first learn how to use their own instruments—that is, their bodies and minds—and then focus that training on the details of their roles in each of the grove ceremonies.

The basic training in playing the "instrument" of AODA's Druid ritual consists of regular practice of the spiritual exercises taught to Candidate members—above all, the Sphere of Protection, the basic ritual practice of the order's study program. The AODA recommends that all its members practice the Sphere of Protection daily; there are many good reasons for this recommendation, but one of them is that it provides solid training for future grove officers.

On the physical level, daily practice of any ritual teaches the practitioner the art of combining concentration, imagination, and intention with gestures and words in a ritual context; on a mental level, the Sphere of Protection teaches the student to imagine the symbolic cosmos used in AODA ritual work and connect with the energies of the four material elements and the three forms of spirit. In addition, of course, this ritual is performed in the opening of every grove or study group meeting, and all present need to be able to participate in building up the imagery and the intentions while it is being performed.

When the Sphere of Protection has been practiced daily for a year or more, the next stage in the training consists of learning a solitary version of the grove opening and closing ritual, and practicing this regularly—at least once a week. When this has been learned well, the next step consists of learning and practicing a version of the

Candidate initiation designed to be performed by a single initiator. Beyond the training these rituals give in the structure and energetics of grove work, they also have a specific and important purpose, which is to prepare the student to confer the Candidate initiation when there is no grove or study group available to do so, or when a grove or study group does not yet have a sufficient number of trained officers to do the work of initiation properly. The First and Second Degree rituals may also be conferred in sole initiator form, and the rituals are made available to qualified members for this purpose; the Third Degree is only conferred by members of the Grand Grove.

There are many other exercises and practices that can be used to prepare for office in a grove or study group, either on one's own or in a group setting; almost anything that helps build the ability to combine physical motions and spoken words with imagination and intention will help build the necessary skills. Perhaps the best approach once the Sphere of Protection, the solitary grove ritual, and the sole initiator form of the Candidate initiation have been mastered, though, is to imagine yourself taking part in a grove meeting as one of the officers. Take the time to build up the imaginary grove as clearly as possible in your imagination; enter the grove through the gate proper to your grade, take your place, and go through the entire opening and closing ritual in your imagination as though you were taking part in a working grove on the material plane.

As with any other kind of work with the imagination, the more senses you add to the experience and the more vividly you imagine them, the better the results will be. Thus it's important not only to see the actions and movements but to hear the words and raps of the Chief Druid's staff, smell the incense and other scents, and so on. Done in this manner, such practices will make it relatively easy to step into a role in an actual grove or study group meeting and do the ritual work with a minimum of fumbling and a maximum of effect.

The Druid Grove Handbook

The Sphere of Protection

The Sphere of Protection was created in the 1970s by Dr. John Gilbert, then one of the Order's archdruids, using material drawn from several older rituals. The Sphere has three phases: an opening, a closing, and a middle section in which the core work is done. The opening is called the Elemental Cross, the middle section is the Calling of the Elements, and the closing is the Sphere of Light.

The process of learning the Sphere of Protection involves a certain degree of complexity, because each person who learns and practices it is expected to enrich it with personally relevant symbolism. The details of the learning process are covered in The Druid Magic Handbook. The version given here is an example rather than a specific form to be followed letter by letter, and the particular set of divine names names and symbols may be used but are not mandatory; readers familiar with other forms of the same ritual will find that the one given here differs from these others in several respects.

The wording that invokes the blessing of the elements for the grove, however, should be used either as given or with minor modifications in grove workings, and the invocation of the telluric, solar, and lunar currents should not be changed in grove workings unless the student has very good reason to do so. The three currents are the main sources of power in AODA grove ritual, and the Sphere of Protection ritual is the way these powers are called into the grove and linked to its symbolism and ceremonial formulae.

1. The Elemental Cross

(To begin this version of the Sphere, stand at the altar—at the south side of the altar, facing north, when performing the ritual in a grove meeting; at the north side of the altar, facing south, in a solitary grove practice; in the center of the room, facing south, in a solitary practice of the Sphere of Protection alone. Imagine the Sun standing at zenith high above your head, and an equivalent sphere of silver-green fire, which the heart of the Earth, far below your feet.

65

Be aware of yourself standing between these two spheres.

Now bring your arms up from your sides in an arc, bringing them together above your head. Imagine a ray of light descending from the Sun to your hands. Draw the hands down to your forehead, joining palm to palm, and imagine the light descending with the movement to form a sphere of light, like a star, within your head. As your hands pause before your forehead, say:)

Hu the Mighty, Great Druid God.

(Draw the hands down to the region of your solar plexus, keeping the palms joined. Imagine the light descending to your solar plexus, and forming a second sphere of light there, then descending through you and beyond you to the sphere of fire at the heart of the Earth. As your hands pause at your solar plexus, say:)

Hesus of the Oaks, Chief of Tree-Spirits.

(Leaving your left hand where it is, at your solar plexus, pivot your right arm outwards at the elbow, so that your right arm ends up angling down and outwards in a straight line from your shoulder. Imagine a ray of light shooting out from the sphere of light at your solar plexus into infinite distance to your right. Say:)

Ceridwen the Wise, Keeper of the Cauldron.

(Repeat the same gesture with your left hand, so that both arms now slope down and outward from your shoulders, forming with your body the image of the Three Rays. Imagine a ray of light shooting out from the sphere of light at your solar plexus into infinite distance to your left. Say:)

Niwalen of the Flowers, Child of Spring.

(Cross your arms across your chest, right over left, and imagine twin rays of light shooting out from the sphere of light at your solar plexus in front of you and behind you into infinite distance. Say:)

May the powers of Nature bless and protect this grove, this day and always.

(This completes the Elemental Cross.)

2. The Calling of the Elements

(Go to the eastern quarter of the grove, and trace the symbol

66

of the element of air, which is a circle with a line extending straight upwards from its uppermost point. Trace the circle first, clockwise from the uppermost point, then trace the line; this is the summoning mode of drawing the symbol. Imagine the symbol being traced in a line of golden light, and the circle filling in with golden light.

(As you do so, imagine a scene beyond the symbol corresponding to the symbolism of the east—for example, a spring meadow at daybreak with the Sun rising, a fresh wind blowing toward you with the scent of grass and flowers, great billowing clouds in the distance with their edges turned golden by the Sun's rays, and so on. Say:)

By the yellow gate of the rushing winds and the hawk of May in the heights of morning, I invoke the air, its gods, its spirits, and its powers. May the powers of Air bless and protect this grove, and further its work.

(Now trace the same symbol again, but trace the circle counterclockwise from the uppermost point, then draw the line upwards as before; this is the banishing mode of drawing the symbol. Say:)

I thank the air for its gifts. And with the help of the powers of air, I banish from within and around this grove all harmful and disturbing influences and every imbalance of the nature of air. I banish these things far from this place.

(Go to the southern quarter of the grove, and trace the symbol of the element of fire, which is an equilateral triangle, point up Trace this clockwise from the uppermost point to summon; imagine the symbol being drawn in red light, then filled in with red light.

(As you do so, imagine a scene beyond the symbol corresponding to the symbolism of the south—for example, a desert like those in the American southwest at noon on a summer's day, with red rock mesas in the middle distance and reddish sand close by, the sun blazing down overhead, the heat making the air shimmer and radiating toward you, and so on. Say:)

By the red gate of the bright flames and the white stag of the summer greenwood, I invoke the fire, its gods, its spirits, and its powers. May the powers of fire bless and protect this grove, and further its work.

(Now trace the same symbol again, counterclockwise from the uppermost point, to banish. Say:)

I thank the fire for its gifts. And with the help of the powers of fire, I banish from within and around this grove all harmful and disturbing influences and every imbalance of the nature of fire. I banish these things far from this place.

(Go to the western quarter of the grove, and trace the symbol of the element of water, which is an equilateral triangle, point down. Trace this clockwise from the lowermost point to summon; imagine the symbol being drawn in blue light, then filled in with blue light.

(As you do so, imagine a scene beyond the symbol corresponding to the symbolism of the west—for example, an ocean beach at sunset on an autumn day, with great waves rolling toward you from out of the distance, rain falling from clouds overhead, the sun blazing down overhead, the setting sun just visible on the horizon through a gap in the clouds and its rays making the clouds and sea glow, and so on. Say:)

By the blue gate of the mighty waters and the salmon of wisdom in the sacred pool, I invoke the water, its gods, its spirits, and its powers. May the powers of water bless and protect this grove, and further its work.

(Now trace the same symbol again, counterclockwise from the lowermost point, to banish. Say:)

I thank the water for its gifts. And with the help of the powers of water, I banish from within and around this grove all harmful and disturbing influences and every imbalance of the nature of water. I banish these things far from this place.

(Go to the southern quarter of the grove, and trace the symbol of the element of earth, which is a circle with a line extending down from its lowermost point—the mirror image of the symbol of air. Trace the clockwise from the lowermost point, and then draw the line downward, to summon; imagine the symbol being drawn in green light, then filled in with green light.

(As you do so, imagine a scene beyond the symbol corresponding to the symbolism of the north—for example, a forest scene at midnight in winter, with snow on the ground and the trees, the moon and stars shining brilliantly in a clear night sky, distant mountains beyond them with their peaks illuminated by the moonlihgt, and so on. Say:)

By the green gate of the tall stones and the great bear of the starry heavens, I invoke the earth, its gods, its spirits, and its powers. May the powers of earth bless and protect this grove, and further its work.

(Now trace the same symbol again, drawing the circle counterclockwise from the lowermost point and then the line down from it, to banish. Say:)

I thank the earth for its gifts. And with the help of the powers of earth, I banish from within and around this grove all harmful and disturbing influences and every imbalance of the nature of earth. I banish these things far from this place.

(Go to the north of the altar and face south. Trace a clockwise circle above the altar; imagine it traced in orange light, the rich orange of autumn leaves, and then fill it with the same color. Then imagine the circle descending through the altar until it is several yards down into the earth beneath you.

(As you do this, imagine the soil and stone beneath you, reaching down all the way to the green fire at the Earth's heart. Feel its stability, its richness, its immense and unhuman power. and so on. Say:)

By the orange gate of the land beneath this grove and the power of the telluric current, I invoke Spirit Below, its gods, its spirits, and its powers. May a ray of the telluric current bless and protect this grove, and further its work.

(Imagine a ray of silver-green flame rising up from the earth's center to the altar, coming to a halt just below the altar's surface. Say:)

I thank Spirit Below for its gifts.

(Trace a clockwise circle in the air high above the altar, imagining it traced in purple light, and then fill it with the same color. Then imagine the circle rising up in the air until it is several yards above the altar.

(As you do this, imagine the heavens above you, luminous with stars and galaxies, extending up beyond the reach of your mind's eye.

Feel its beauty, its silence, its vastness, and so on. Say:)

By the purple gate of the skies above this grove, and the power of the solar current, I invoke Spirit Above, its gods, its spirits, and its powers. May a ray of the solar current bless and protect this grove, and further its work.

(Imagine a ray of golden light from the Sun up above you, descending to the altar, and coming to a halt just above the altar's surface. Say:)

I thank Spirit Above for its gifts.

(Now be aware of the six symbols of the elements in the six directions of space surrounding the grove. Say:)

By the six powers here invoked and here present, and by the grand word by which the worlds were made—

AWEN (chanting this word as before, Ah-Oh-En)

—I invoke Spirit Within. May a ray of the lunar current bless and protect this grove, and further its work.

(If you are in a grove, touch the mistletoe on the sickle with your right hand.)

May it establish a sphere of protection around this grove and all within it.

(This completes the Calling of the Elements.)

3. The Sphere of Light

(This phase of the ritual uses words and gestures only at its conclusion. The rest of the work is done solely by the imagination.

(Imagine the solar and telluric currents coming into contact at the top of the altar and forming a sphere of brilliant white light that surrounds the altar top and includes the four cauldrons. See the colored light from each cauldron radiating into the larger sphere of white light, so that it shimmers with rainbow colors.

(Next, imagine the sphere of light expanding outward until it surrounds the grove and all within it. Take your time at this visualization, and build up the image as strongly and solidly as you are able. Concentrate on the idea that the sphere forms a barrier impenetrable to any hostile or harmful influence, a protective wall within which the work of the grove may go on unhindered.

(When you have established the sphere as firmly as you can, cross your arms across your chest and say:)

I thank the powers for their blessings.

(Then proceed to the work of the grove, if the ritual is being done as part of a grove ceremony, or if the Sphere of Protection is being practiced by itself, pause for a few minutes, feeling the energies you have invoked, and then release the imagery from your mind, write up the experience in your practice journal, and go on with your day.)

Solitary Grove Ceremony

The solitary grove ceremony is an adaptation and simplification of the standard AODA grove opening and closing. For best results, it should be done in a room or other place where there is ample room to move around an altar set up in the center. The altar itself may be anything from a purpose-built wooden structure to a folding TV tray draped with a white cloth; it should have the four cauldrons on it—one with incense in the east, one with a candle or lamp in the south, one with water in the west, and one with salt in the north. (The cauldrons with incense and flame should have a layer of clean sand in the bottom for insulation from the heat.)

The other items you will need are a chair; a sword, preferably straight and double-edged, if you can get one; a sickle; and a spray of mistletoe if this can be provided—the small packets sold for the holidays are perfectly suitable for this—or some other plant if mistletoe is not an option. The chair is set on the northern edge of the circle, facing the altar; the sword is in a convenient place close to the chair; the sickle and mistletoe are in the middle of the altar, facing whatever direction corresponds to your degree of initiation.

Solitary Grove Opening

(Before beginning a ceremony, put the altar cloth and any decorations on the altar, and arrange the four cauldrons. Light the incense and the lamp, and then go to the edge of the area where you'll be performing the ceremony. Take a few moments to clear your mind of unrelated thoughts and feelings.

(Then, when you are ready to begin, enter the circle through whichever gate your degree entitles you to use, then go around to the north side of the altar, where you face south. Raise your right hand palm forward to salute the Spiritual Sun, which is always symbolically at high noon in the southern sky, and say:)

Let the powers be attentive as I am about to open a Grove of Druids in this place. The first duty of Druids assembled in the Sacred Grove is to proclaim peace to the four quarters of the world,

The Druid Grove Handbook

for without peace our work cannot proceed.

(Take the sword from its place, still sheathed, and circle around to the east. Face outward and raise the sword in its sheath, holding it horizontally at head level, right hand on hilt, left on sheath. Draw the sword partway from the sheath so that half the blade is visible, then push the sword back into the sheath; if you have no sword, raise your right hand palm outward to salute each direction instead. Say:)

I proclaim peace in the east.

(Lower the sword and proceed to the south, where you repeat the same process, drawing the sword partway and then sheathing it, saying:)

I proclaim peace in the south.

(Proceed to the west, and do the same thing, saying:)

I proclaim peace in the west.

(Proceed to the north and do the same thing, saying:)

I proclaim peace in the north.

(Return the sword to its place and advance to the north side of the altar, facing south across it. Say:)

The four quarters are at peace and the work of the grove may proceed. Let this grove and all within it be purified with air.

(Go to the eastern side of the altar, pick up the cauldron with the incense, and carry it to the eastern edge of the space. Pause there, holding the cauldron out as though offering the incense, and then walk in a clockwise circle once around the outer edge of the space, tracing a circle around the grove with the cauldron. When you've come back around to the east, return the cauldron to the altar.

(While you do this, visualize the following. When you hold the cauldron as though offering the incense, imagine a current of yellow light streaming in from the east and forming a sphere of yellow light around the cauldron. As you carry the cauldron around the grove, imagine the cauldron tracing a line of yellow light in a circle around the outside of the grove. When you carry the cauldron back to the altar, see it trace a line of yellow light in from the edge to the altar, and see the sphere of yellow light remaining with the cauldron on the altar.

(When you have finished, say:)

73

Let this Grove and all within it be purified with fire.

(Go to the southern side of the altar, pick up the cauldron with the flame, and carry it to the southern edge of the space. Pause there, holding the cauldron out as though offering the flame, and then walk in a clockwise circle once around the outer edge of the space, tracing a circle around the grove with the cauldron. When you've come back around to the south, return the cauldron to the altar.

(While you do this, visualize the following. When you hold the cauldron as though offering the incense, imagine a current of red light streaming in from the south and forming a sphere of red light around the cauldron. As you carry the cauldron around the grove, imagine the cauldron tracing a line of red light in a circle around the outside of the grove. When you carry the cauldron back to the altar, see it trace a line of red light in from the edge to the altar, and see the sphere of red light remaining with the cauldron on the altar.

(When you have finished, say:)

Let this Grove and all within it be purified with water.

(Go to the western side of the altar, pick up the cauldron with the water, and carry it to the western edge of the space. Pause there, holding the cauldron out as though offering the water, and then walk in a clockwise circle once around the outer edge of the space, tracing a circle around the grove with the cauldron. When you've come back around to the west, return the cauldron to the altar.

(While you do this, visualize the following. When you hold the cauldron as though offering the water, imagine a current of blue light streaming in from the west and forming a sphere of blue light around the cauldron. As you carry the cauldron around the grove, imagine the cauldron tracing a line of blue light in a circle around the outside of the grove. When you carry the cauldron back to the altar, see it trace a line of blue light in from the edge to the altar, and see the sphere of blue light remaining with the cauldron on the altar.

(When you have finished, say:)

Let this Grove and all within it be purified with earth.

(Go to the northern side of the altar, pick up the cauldron with the salt, and carry it to the northern edge of the space. Pause there, holding the cauldron out as though offering the salt, and then walk in a clockwise circle once around the outer edge of the space, tracing a circle around the grove with the cauldron from north to north. When you've come back around to the north, return the cauldron to the altar.

(While you do this, visualize the following. When you hold the cauldron as though offering the salt, imagine a current of green light streaming in from the north and forming a sphere of green light around the cauldron. As you carry the cauldron around the grove, imagine the cauldron tracing a line of green light in a circle around the outside of the grove. When you carry the cauldron back to the altar, see it trace a line of green light in from the edge to the altar, and see the sphere of green light remaining with the cauldron on the altar.

(When you have finished, say:)

I invoke the blessing of the holy powers with the words that have been the bond among all Druids:

Grant, O holy ones, thy protection;

And in protection, strength;

And in strength, understanding;

And in understanding, knowledge;

And in knowledge, the knowledge of justice;

And in the knowledge of justice, the love of it;

And in that love, the love of all existences;

And in the love of all existences, the love of Earth our mother and all goodness.

(When you've finished the prayer, chant the word Awen three times:)

AWEN, AWEN, AWEN

(Draw the word out into its three syllables – Ah-Oh-En – and let it resonate throughout your body and the Grove. Then perform the complete Sphere of Protection ceremony to complete the opening of the grove.

(When this is finished go to the chair in the north and take your seat. This completes the opening ceremony.)

Solitary Grove Closing

(When the work of the Grove is completed, sit down in the chair in the north and let your mind return to stillness. When you're ready, rise and go to the north side of the altar, facing south across it. Say:)

Let the powers be attentive as I am about to close a grove of Druids in this place.

(Go to the eastern side of the altar. Take the cauldron with the incense to the east, and hold it outward as though offering the incense, as in the opening. Say:)

With thanks I release the powers of air to their rightful places. May peace prevail in the east.

(As you say this, imagine the yellow light that surrounds the cauldron flowing back to its sources in the east. When this is finished, return the cauldron to its place on the altar, and go to the southern side of the altar. Take the cauldron with the flame to the south, and hold it outward as though offering the flame, as in the opening. Say:)

With thanks I release the powers of fire to their rightful places. May peace prevail in the south.

(As you say this, imagine the red light that surrounds the cauldron flowing back to its sources in the south. When this is finished, return the cauldron to its place on the altar, and go to the western side of the altar. Take the cauldron with the water to the west, and hold it outward as though offering the water, as in the opening. Say:)

With thanks I release the powers of water to their rightful places. May peace prevail in the west.

(As you say this, imagine the blue light that surrounds the cauldron flowing back to its sources in the west. When this is finished, return the cauldron to its place on the altar, and go to the northern side of the altar. Take the cauldron with the salt to the north, and hold it outward as though offering the salt, as in the opening. Say:)

With thanks I release the powers of earth to their rightful places. May peace prevail in the north.

(As you say this, imagine the green light that surrounds the cauldron flowing back to its sources in the north. When this is finished, return the cauldron to its place on the altar, and remain at the northern side of the altar, facing south. Say:)

Peace prevails in the four quarters and throughout the grove. Let any power remaining from this working be returned to the Earth for her blessing.

(Any ritual working leaves some energy behind it, and this can usually be sensed as a mood, a feeling, or a subtle sense of presence in the space. Imagine this flowing inward toward the altar, down through it to the earth, and then down to the earth's center. Keep concentrating on this until the ritual space feels clear of any leftover energy. Then say:)

I now invoke the Sword of Swords.

(If you have a sword, draw it and hold it high with the hilt up and the point down. If you don't have one, visualize a great medieval sword in that position, hovering in the air before you, and raise your hand in salute. Say the following incantation:)

From the rising Sun, three rays of light;

From the living Earth, three stones of witness;

From the eye and the mind and the hand of wisdom, three rowan staves of all knowledge.

From the fire of the Sun, the forge;

From the bones of the Earth, the steel;

From the hand of the wise, the making:

From these, Excalibur.

By the Sword of Swords, I pledge my faithful service to the living Earth, our home and mother.

(Chant the word Awen once, drawing out the syllables Ah-Oh-En:)

AWEN.

(As you chant the word, imagine the sword—whether physical or imagined—dissolving into pure light, which draws together into the image of the Sun, standing at the zenith in the south. Lower the sword, sheath it, and put it back in its place, or lower your hand, and leave the altar; walk in a clockwise circle around the grove to whichever gate your degree entitles you to use, and exit the grove.

This concludes the closing ceremony.)

Initiation of a Candidate
(Sole Initiator Form)

This version of the Candidate initiation is designed to be performed by a single initiator, in situations when a grove or study group cannot be convened. It should be learned, practiced, and if possible memorized by every Second Degree initiate of the order, both so that new members of the order may be provided with the experience of ceremonial initiation, and so that present and prospective chief Druids of study groups and groves can familiarize themselves with the structure of the ritual and be better prepared to confer it in its full form when circumstances permit.

Before the following ritual begins, the grove should be opened using the Solitary Grove Opening (pp. 52-54). There should be an anteroom or other place for the candidate to wait outside the grove for the duration of the opening ceremony.

(Before the ceremony, the anteroom is decorated with green boughs, if possible, to represent a clearing in the forest, and images of the Paths in the Forest are set up, if available. Once the Candidate is in the anteroom, the grove is opened in regular form, and all lights are turned down, with only the altar at the center of the grove illuminated. A yellow cord belt of appropriate length for the candidate is in readiness near the altar.)

(When all is ready, Initiator proceeds to the anteroom to greet the Candidate.)

Initiator: Be welcome in our Druid Grove. Come with me. I will be your Guide as you decide if you truly wish to become a Druid - or not.

(Initiator takes Candidate by the left arm, leads Candidate into the Grove , and proceeds to a position just South of the Altar, facing North.)

Initiator: Please kneel at the altar, and call silently upon Deity, by whatever name or form you prefer, and ask for guidance as you decide whether to follow the Path of a Druid or not. When you are finished, please say aloud: "So mote it be," and await my return.

Candidate: (after praying) So mote it be.

(Initiator comes to Candidate's side quickly, takes candidate by the left arm and helps her/him to arise.)

Initiator: Come with me.

(Initiator takes Candidate out through the eastern gate of the grove, and back to the anteroom.)

Initiator: There are many paths in life. The path you have been following is that traveled by most people in this life. If you continue to follow it, you will work hard at honest work, raise a family if you will and Deity permits, and meet with your friends in the mead hall to tell tall tales and brag of worthless victories. Your life will be full of happiness and sadness, joy and peace, fear and anger, pain and suffering, love, apathy and hate. This is the Path of Ignorance and it leads you in a circle back to this Place of Decision time after time, life after life.

(Initiator points to another path.)

This is the well-worn path of successful people who as craftsmen and artisans earn their keep. They are more prosperous than ordinary working folk but they travel a rocky road of feast or famine. They enjoy happiness, peace, love and joy and they also suffer sadness, fear, anger, pain, hatred and apathy. Even though they are more prosperous than most, they also follow a Path of Ignorance.

(Initiator points to another path.)

This path covered with brambles and difficult to see is the Path of Leadership which few are willing to travel. It is a difficult path because leaders must clear the path so others may follow. This path leads to riches and privileges impossibleto imagine. Great leaders and various scoundrels follow this Path of Ignorance that also leads to sadness and happiness, anger and fear, pain and suffering, joy and peace, love, apathy and hatred.

(Initiator points to several other paths)

These are all paths leading to success in this world and all of them are Paths of Ignorance. There is one more path before you. It is the Path of Knowledge. It is a difficult path, filled with hard work both within yourself and in this world you see before you. It is a path that tests your faith and determination constantly. It tests you in every relationship you enter and in every decision you make.

If you pass these tests, you will attain everything you can attain on any other path and you will attain knowledge. You will attain knowledge about the Sun and the Moon, the Earth and the sky, all the stars in the canopy of heaven and all the grains of sand on Mother Earth. You will attain knowledge of all the rocks, plants and animals. And you will attain the greatest knowledge of all, the knowledge of yourself.

If you fail these tests, you will return to this place, the Place of Decision so you may choose another path for your life. I will leave you here in this Place of Decision for you to decide which path you want to travel. Choose any path and I will still be your friend. But should you choose to discover the Path of Knowledge, return to the Grove and knock thrice upon the portal, and you will be admitted. I will await you until the Sun rises again in the East.

(Initiator returns to grove, leaving candidate in anteroom. When Candidate knocks thrice on the portal of the grove, Initiator goes to meet him/her.)

Initiator: Be welcome once more in the Grove of the Druids. You have chosen to follow the Path of Knowledge for now. If that is your true intention, please kneel at the altar and once again ask for the guidance of Deity. When you have completed your silent prayer, signal as before by saying "So mote it be."

(Initiator leads Candidate to altar, assists her/him to kneel, and then steps back a few paces.)

Candidate: So mote it be. (The Candidate remains kneeling.)

Initiator: (rises) As your initiator it falls to me to ask several questions concerning your intentions. Answer me truly. Is it your desire to follow the Path of Knowledge and learn the secrets of a Druid? If this is not your desire, say "No" and leave this Grove. I will leave with you as a sign of our friendship. But if it is your desire, say "Yes" and we will continue.

(Candidate answers)

Initiator: The first steps of the Path of Knowledge will require you to learn from Earth and Sun and Moon for one year: to learn the ways of nature along the Earth Path, to celebrate the cycles of nature along the Sun Path, and to explore the mysteries of your own nature along the Moon Path. Are you willing to study these Paths for one year, to learn what they have to teach you? If you are not so willing, say "No" and leave this Grove. I will leave with you as a sign of our friendship. But if you are so willing, say "Yes" and we will continue.

(Candidate answers.)

Initiator: The river that is Druidry has three great currents: the way of the Ovate, the student of nature; the way of the Bard, the student of the arts; and the way of the Druid, the student of the spirit. As part of your first steps along the Path of Knowledge, you will be required to choose one or more of these currents and undertake an exploration into their lore and wisdom. Are you willing to make such an exploration? If you are not so willing, say "No" and leave this Grove. I will leave with you as a sign of our friendship. But if you are so willing, say "Yes" and we will continue.

(Candidate answers)

Initiator: You have answered "yes" to every question. If that is your intention you may proceed. If that is not your intention, you may not proceed and we will leave this sacred grove together as friends. Do you wish to proceed?

(Candidate answers. If all the answers have been affirmative, the ceremony proceeds.)

Initiator: Arise, Candidate (name).

(Initiator assists in helping Candidate to his/her feet.)

Initiator: In the name and under the authority of the Grand Grove of the Ancient Order of Druids in America I proclaim you and welcome you as a Candidate of our Order.

(Initiator helps Candidate put on cord belt.)

Now we begin a journey through the realms of the elements. Listen carefully to the instruction you will receive.

(Initiator takes Candidate by the left arm and proceeds to the Northeast part of the circle.)

Initiator: Among Druids the place in which we meet is termed a grove. As a Candidate your place in this grove and every grove will be in the Northeast. Here you will be close to the Eastern Gate through which you are to enter and leave the Grove. Only those of higher degrees may freely enter and leave by the other gates. As a Candidate your gate is always in the East.

(Initiator and Candidate reach the East Gate.)

Initiator: This is the East Gate. It is the Yellow Gate of Alban Eiler, the Gate of the Rushing Winds, through which you may enter and leave this Grove as a Candidate. It is your privilege as a Candidate to pass through this Gate.

In our teachings, the mysteries of the elements are resumed in the Sphere of Protection, which is the first ritual you are instructed to learn and practice, and the key to most of the secrets of our Order. You will begin your instruction in that ritual here, in the east, by facing east. Trace a circle before you in the air clockwise, beginning thus at the uppermost point (does so), imagining it drawn in a line of yellow flame. Draw a line of yellow flame upwards from the uppermost point of the circle (does so) to complete the symbol of air. Imagine the circle filled with yellow flame and, pointing to the center, say, "I invoke the powers of air and ask for their blessing." Do this now.

(Candidate does so)

Initiator: Now trace the same symbol again, but draw the circle counterclockwise. Point to the center and say, "And with the help of the powers of air I banish all hostile influences from this place." Do this now.

(Candidate follows these instructions, prompted as necessary.)

Initiator: It is well. We now pass on to the quarter of fire.

(Initiator and Candidate proceed to the South Gate.)

Initiator: This is the South Gate. It is the Red Gate of Alban Heruin, the Gate of the Bright Flames, through which Druid Apprentices enter and leave this Grove. It is your aspiration as a Candidate to pass through this Gate.

You will continue your instruction in the Sphere of Protection here, in the south, by facing south. Trace a triangle point upwards before you in the air clockwise, beginning it thus from the uppermost point (does so), imagining it drawn in a line of red flame. Imagine the triangle filled with red flame and, pointing to the center, say, "I invoke the powers of fire and ask for their blessing." Do this now.

(Candidate does so)

Initiator: Now trace the same symbol again, but draw the triangle counterclockwise. Point to the center and say, "And with the help of the powers of fire I banish all hostile influences from this place." Do this now.

(Candidate follows these instructions, prompted as necessary.)

Initiator: It is well. We now pass on to the quarter of water.

(Initiator and Candidate proceed to the West Gate.)

Initiator: This is the Blue Gate of Alban Elued, the Gate of the Mighty Waters, through which the Druid Companions and Druid Adepts enter and leave this Grove. It is your task as a Candidate to learn from those who pass through this gate.

You will continue your instruction in the Sphere of Protection here, in the west, by facing west. Trace a triangle point downwards before you in the air clockwise, beginning it thus from the lowermost point (does so), imagining it drawn in a line of blue flame. Imagine the triangle filled with blue flame and, pointing to the center, say, "I invoke the powers of water and ask for their blessing." Do this now.

(Candidate does so)

Initiator: Now trace the same symbol again, but draw the triangle counterclockwise. Point to the center and say, "And with the help of the powers of water I banish all hostile influences from this place." Do this now.

(Candidate follows these instructions, prompted as necessary.)

Initiator: It is well. We now pass on to the quarter of Earth.

(Initiator and Candidate proceed to the North Gate.)

Initiator: This is the North Gate. It is the Green Gate of Alban Arthuan, the Gate of the Tall Stones, through which only the Ever-Living Ones, our guardian spirits and the messengers of Deity, may enter and leave this grove. It is your duty as a Candidate to offer due reverence to those who pass through this gate.

You will continue your instruction in the Sphere of Protection

The Druid Grove Handbook

here, in the north, by facing north. Trace a circle before you in the air clockwise, beginning it thus at the lowermost point (dces so), imagining it drawn in a line of green flame. Draw a line of green flame downwards from the lowermost point of the circle (does so) to complete the symbol of earth. Imagine the circle filled with green flame and, pointing to the center, say, "I invoke the powers cf earth and ask for their blessing." Do this now.

(Candidate does so)

Initiator: Now trace the same symbol again, but draw the circle counterclockwise. Point to the center and say, "And with the help of the powers of earth I banish all hostile influences from this place." Do this now.

(Candidate follows these instructions, promp:ed as necessary.)

Initiator: It is well. We now pass on to the altar, the heart of the grove, to learn the mysteries of Spirit.

(Initiator and Candidate proceed back to the East Gate, then to the altar.)

Initiator: We return to the place of beginnings, and then to the center of this grove. This is the place of the Orange, Violet, and White Gates of the Spirit. In the depth of the Earth stands the Gate Below and the Ray of Power. In the heights of heaven stands the Gate Above and the Ray of Knowledge. In the center of all stands the Gate Within and the Ray of Peace. These three rays of light are always present in the grove, and in any other place where you may be, for by them all things came into being.

You will complete your instruction in the Sphere of Protection here, at the center. In any grove in which you do not preside, you will approach the altar always from the south. Trace a circle ir the air over the altar top before you, imagining it drawn in orange flame, and say: "I invoke the powers of Spirit Below and ask for their blessing." Do this now.

(Candidate does so.)

Now trace a circle in the air above you, imagining it drawn in violet flame, and say: "I invoke the powers of Spirit Above and ask for their blessing." Do this now.

(Candidate does so.)

Now touch your heart, imagining white radiance shining out in all directions, and say, "I invoke the powers of Spirit Within. May a Sphere of Protection be established about me now and always." Do this now.

(Candidate does so. Initiator and Candidate then proceed to the northeast quarter of the grove.)

Initiator: This Sphere of Protection will protect you from harm and deception this day. You will be given written instructions on how to perform this ritual daily to protect yourself and any place you may be. It will keep you safe while you study the things you have promised to study and learn. My blessings go with you on your journey, and the help of those who pass through all four gates of the Grove will be available to you should you need it. Study and learn no matter what may befall you. Take your place in the Northeast.

(Candidate is seated in the Northeast. The grove is closed in solitary form.)

The Druid Grove Handbook

For further information about
the Ancient Order of Druids in America,
please write to:

PO Box 996,
Cumberland MD 21501

or visit our website at http://www.aoda.org

www.ingramcontent.com/pod-product-compliance
Lightning Source LLC
Chambersburg PA
CBHW032023090426

42741CB00006B/719